TREASURY OF THE WORLD

TREASURY OF THE WORLD

Jewelled Arts of India in the Age of the Mughals

MANUEL KEENE

with

SALAM KAOUKJI

Thames & Hudson

in association with

The al-Sabah Collection

Dar al-Athar al-Islamiyyah, Kuwait National Museum

ITINERARY OF THE 'TREASURY OF THE WORLD' EXHIBITION
The British Museum, London: May 2001
The Metropolitan Museum of Art, New York: October 2001
Cleveland Museum of Art: February 2002
The Museum of Fine Arts, Houston: June 2002
Los Angeles County Museum of Art: December 2002

Cover photographs by Edward Owen (*front*) and Bruce White (*back*)

On the cover
Front: Dish [detail]. Mughal, *c.* 1st quarter 17th century AD.
LNS 1785 J. Cat. no. 13.2
Back: Pendant with cameo portrait of the emperor Shah Jahan.
Mughal, *c.* 6th decade 17th century AD.
LNS 43 J. Cat. no. 9.11

Frontispiece
Dish [enlarged]. Mughal, *c.* 1st quarter 17th century AD.
LNS 1785 J. Cat. no. 13.2

Page 8
Water-pipe reservoir (*huqqa*) [detail].
Probably Deccan or Western India, later 16th–early 17th century AD.
LNS 2174 Ja. Cat. no. 3.2

Page 11
Pendant with cameo portrait of the emperor Shah Jahan [detail].
Mughal, *c.* 6th decade 17th century AD.
LNS 43 J. Cat. no. 9.11

Page 12
Inscribed royal spinel ('balas ruby') [detail].
Inscription of Ulugh Beg (before AD 1449).
LNS 1660 J. Cat. no. 12.1
(Photomicrograph by Manuel Keene)

First published in the United Kingdom in 2001 by Thames & Hudson Ltd,
181A High Holborn, London WC1V 7QX
www.thamesandhudson.com

British Library Cataloguing-in-Publication Data
A catalogue record for this book is available from the British Library

ISBN 0-500-97608-2

Designed by Maggi Smith

Printed and bound in Singapore by C.S. Graphics

CONTENTS

Sir Thomas Roe was England's first ambassador (1615–19) to the court of the 'Great Mogul'.
In a letter to Prince Charles, later King Charles I, dated 30 October 1616,
he wrote of the emperor Jahangir:

In jewells (which is one of his felicityes)
hee is the treasury of the world,
buyeing all that comes, and heaping rich stones
as if hee would rather build then weare them.

The quotation above is taken from Foster, William, ed.,
The Embassy of Sir Thomas Roe to India 1615–19, New Delhi, 1990
(reprint of the revised 1926 Oxford University Press edition), p. 270.

All pieces in the catalogue are unpublished
except as stated otherwise in the respective entries.

PREFACE

SHEIKH NASSER SABAH AL-AHMAD AL-SABAH

I began to discover my love of historic art during my schooling in Jerusalem in the 1960s. I was particularly enthralled by the monuments of that ancient city, especially her Islamic monuments, which number in the scores and span the 7th to the 20th centuries AD. As part of my own heritage, these filled me with pride and planted the germ of curiosity about the extent of Islamic artistic achievements.

Such awakened consciousness found expression in the inception of my collecting of Islamic art objects in the middle 1970s. From the beginning, I had an urge to share my enthusiasms for these thrilling remains of the past, an urge also shared by my wife and eventual director of our museum, Sheikha Hussah Sabah al-Salim al-Sabah. Our efforts culminated in the installation of this collection in its own building of the Kuwait National Museum Complex, opening in February 1983, where it was housed and exhibited up to the Iraqi invasion in 1990. The Collection was and is of a broad and comprehensive nature, and has continued to be augmented over the years up to the present.

My special love of the jewelled arts meant that, from the beginning, Islamic, and especially Indian, jewelry formed a particularly active branch of my collecting, which has continued at a generally increasing intensity over all those years. As my collection grew, so, naturally, did my awareness, and the selection process became more refined.

A very great problem connected with a desire to collect early and important Indian jewelry is that, unlike other branches of art, there were few existing collections or publications for education and guidance, and one had little to follow but experience and a feel for beauty, rarity and quality. Gradually, however, and especially in recent years, the Collection began to reach what one might call a 'critical mass', by which the study of features and aspects of different pieces showed relationships and shed light on a variety of others. This put us in a privileged position of being able to choose objects for acquisition ever more wisely, despite an increasingly competitive atmosphere.

Actually, it was quite natural for me, as a native of the Gulf region, to feel an affinity with India and Indian art, due to a long familiarity with objects which came from the Subcontinent. Indeed, the people of the Gulf have a long familiarity with India herself, a natural and old connection of particular closeness resulting especially from the maritime trade, which goes back to very ancient times and which continued through into the 20th century. There was even a particular and important jewelry-industry connection in the form of our Gulf pearls, universally recognized as the best ever known, and the most important destination of which was always India.

In the end, however, it is the *art* of Indian jewelry which has attracted me and driven me to explore its dimensions. Acquisition of the best of these works of art prevents their loss or their existence in obscurity, and allows others who are interested to study them. I am confident that making them public in this way, through books and exhibitions, will result in as yet unimagined insights by many scholars and students, and in stimulation of unknown dimensions of a wide range of persons around the world. Such, it seems to me, is an appropriate memorial and heritage for the mostly anonymous artists who will thus have managed, in the pursuit of their profession and livelihood, to bequeath such delight and joy to so many.

FOREWORD

R.G.W. ANDERSON   DIRECTOR, THE BRITISH MUSEUM

The British Museum is honoured to be the inaugural venue of the exhibition 'Treasury of the World: Jewelled Arts of India in the Age of the Mughals' which highlights the superb jewelled objects and gems from the collection of Sheikh Nasser Sabah al-Ahmad al-Sabah of Kuwait. We wish to express our gratitude to Sheikh Nasser for so generously lending this collection and supporting the exhibition. The British Museum is also indebted to Her Majesty Queen Elizabeth II for lending the famed 'Timur Ruby', in fact a royal Mughal spinel, to be shown with other examples of similar provenance.

That Sheikh Nasser al-Sabah of Kuwait has assembled such an extensive collection of Indian jewelled objects and royal Mughal gems over the past twenty-five years is a testament to his single-minded passion and deep knowledge of this field. Despite the disruption of the Gulf War and removal of almost his whole collection to Iraq, Sheikh Nasser's interest in Mughal jewelry did not waver. The British Museum greatly appreciates the opportunity to show Sheikh Nasser's collection in Europe, where visitors are certain to be dazzled by the skill of the Indian jewellers of the age of the Mughals and the beauty of the objects that they produced. Likewise, audiences at the four American venues – The Metropolitan Museum of Art, the Cleveland Museum of Art, The Museum of Fine Arts,

Houston, and the Los Angeles County Museum of Art – will certainly marvel at the exceptional range and quality of jewelled items in this groundbreaking exhibition.

'Treasury of the World: Jewelled Arts of India in the Age of the Mughals' bears witness to the vast wealth of the Mughal rulers of India and their contemporaries in the smaller Muslim courts of the Deccan, or Central India. Moreover, the gems inscribed with the names of the successive rulers of the 16th and 17th centuries reveal that their importance as markers of royal legitimacy grew with time. Remarkable gems and jewelled objects were not only sought after by the Mughals themselves but also were looted by the Persians in the 1739 Sack of Delhi and subsequently select items were presented to the Russian Tsar and the Ottoman Sultan. For the British, India was the 'jewel in the crown' of the Empire; it was at this time that the most famous of Indian jewels were acquired by Queen Victoria and later passed on to Queen Alexandra, Queen Mary and Queen Elizabeth II. The collection of Sheikh Nasser al-Sabah carries on the traditional association of princely connoisseurs and Indian jewelry and continues to inspire the same awe that visitors to the Mughal court must have felt upon beholding the princes and rulers in all their jewelled finery.

ACKNOWLEDGMENTS

Special thanks for the loan of the important inscribed spinel, exhibited with the al-Sabah Collection material at the British Museum:
Her Most Gracious Majesty Queen Elizabeth the Second and The Royal Collection Trust

Institutions and collections which have given permission for the reproduction of their material as visual reference in the 'Treasury of the World' exhibition:
The David Collection, Copenhagen; the Chester Beatty Library, Dublin; the Art and History Trust, Houston; the Türk ve Islam Eserleri Müzesi, Istanbul; the City Palace, Jaipur; The British Museum, London; the Royal Asiatic Society, London; the Victoria & Albert Museum, London; The Metropolitan Museum of Art, New York; the Bibliothèque Nationale, Paris; the Musée Guimet, Paris; the Institute of Oriental Studies, St Petersburg; the Russian National Library, Academy of Sciences, St Petersburg; the San Diego Museum of Art, San Diego; the Freer Gallery of Art, Washington, D.C.; the Royal Library, Windsor Castle

Mentors who have provided invaluable impetus, guidance and encouragement:
Our parents, Coy Curtis, Helen Marshall, Donald St Clair, Cecil Miller, Gerry Deibler, Angelo Garzio, John Williams, Michael Rogers, Christel Kessler, Richard Ettinghausen, Robert Kulicke, Jean Stark, Ralph Pinder-Wilson, Robert Skelton, Sheikh Nasser Sabah al-Ahmad al-Sabah, Sheikha Hussah Sabah al-Salim al-Sabah

Colleagues who are employed to work on behalf of the Collection:
Muhammad Ali, Jennifer Dinsmore, Frances Halahan, Benjamin Hilario, Aurora Luis, William Luis, Maria Mertzani, Laila Musawi, Kirsty Norman, Robin Sanderson, Lieve Vandenbulcke-Hibler

Colleagues who have volunteered their time and effort to help on the Collection, specifically connected with the exhibition and catalogue:
Randa Finan, Ineke Hamburger, Marie-Hélène Maysounave, Monique de Meuron

Others who have made special efforts and considerations on behalf of the Collection in connection with the project:
Husayn Afshar, Avinash Aggarwal, Harishchandra Aggarwal, Graham Boyce, Maharukh Desai, Parmeshwar Godrej, Ossama al-Kaoukji, Nawabzada Aimaduddin Ahmad Khan of Loharu, Olga Nefedova, Nawab Qazim Ali Khan of Rampur, Begum Noor Banu of Rampur, José Luis Roselló, Marie-Hélène Saad, Sheikha Hussa Sa'd al-Abdallah al-Sabah, Sheikha Sheikha Sabah al-Salim al-Sabah, Abolala Soudavar, Bimal Zaveri, Ramesh Zaveri

Specialist colleagues who have helped with their time, knowledge, facilities under their care, references, publications and the like:
Adel Adamova, David Alexander, Anna Bennett, A. D. H. Bivar, Sheila Canby, Stefano Carboni, Anna Contadini, Derek Content, Vesta Curtis, Layla Diba, David Edge, Oliver Everett, Massumeh Farhad, Christa Fischer, Kjeld von Folsach, M. A. Ghajar, Sidney Goldstein, Leonard Gorelick, V. D. Goryacheva, Navina Haidar, Jørgen Hein, Herbert Horovitz, Théodore Horovitz, Anatoly Ivanov, Jaakko Jaaskelainen, Mohammad-Reza Kargar, Rochelle Kessler, Roger Keverne, Liliane el-Kholi, Haeedeh Laleh, Elizabeth Lambourn, Brendan Lynch, Louise Mackie, Souren Melikian-Chirvani, Veronica Murphy, Mikhail Piotrovsky, Jessica Rawson, Simon Ray, Ellen Reeder, Maria Queiroz Ribeiro, Michael Rogers, Mohammed Saleh, Susan Stronge, Deborah Swallow, Daniel Walker, Rachel Ward, Oliver Watson, Michael Willis, Elaine Wright, Benjamin Zucker

Colleagues who have made extraordinary contributions towards the realization of the exhibition and catalogue:
Manijeh Bayani-Wolpert, Mona El Mamoun, Katie Marsh, Robert Skelton

INTRODUCTION

MANUEL KEENE

THE CATALOGUE AND THE COLLECTION

This volume constitutes the first publication of the 'cream' of the holdings of the most comprehensive and richest collection of Indian jewelled arts in the world, that of Sheikh Nasser Sabah al-Ahmad al-Sabah and Sheikha Hussah Sabah al-Salim al-Sabah.

The present work illustrates and describes every piece in the al-Sabah Collection's 'Treasury of the World' exhibition, identifying each object by catalogue number and by the Collection's registration number; detailing the materials, techniques, measurements, and regional and temporal attribution; recording the source and date of its acquisition by the Collection; and listing any previous publication history. The organization of the catalogue reflects the division of the exhibition into thirteen sections of thematic and technical character, following the various branches of the jewelry arts. Each of these sections is preceded by an introductory essay which places the material in perspective, historically, technically and artistically. A sense of the breadth, beauty and interest of this collection is suggested by the fact that the themes materialized under the various headings range from India's special molecular-bond pure gold settings (kundan), through its sublime hardstone carvings (with one whole section focusing on those inlaid with gold and precious stones) to its celebrated enamelling, gold-inlaid steel and carved gemstones. Other sections are devoted to hammered precious-metal arts, sculptural qualities, and, for example, the presentation of the largest collection of inscribed royal gemstones outside the Iranian National Jewels Treasury.

ORGANIZATION AND CONTENT

Personal and portable art *par excellence*, and all the more enhanced in our appreciation for being made from the noblest and most lasting materials available to human manufacture, jewelry and jewelled objects afford their owners endless opportunities to be edified by their qualities. Those without the good fortune to be able to enjoy the direct contact that characterizes this special relationship are best served if the presentation of such objects in exhibitions and publications provides the widest and closest access to their essential nature,

their every nook and cranny. The desire to give the fullest possible picture of classic Indian jewelry, combined with the custodianship of a collection which is able to do so to a unique degree, lies behind this selection of the maximum amount of material for presentation consistent with the maintenance of clarity in the publication and with the provision of the most intimate access possible in the exhibition.

Any requirement to bring coherent and conducive order to a large number of art objects poses irreconcilable problems; and in the end, especially because of the complexity of individual objects, the choices made tend to involve a great deal of cross-referencing and qualification. Among the most problematic aspects of this phenomenon is the fact that any one object usually incorporates notable features of many kinds which relate it to a whole variety of other objects of various overall natures or general aspects, often involving quite different materials or functions. It must be emphasized that the corpus presented here is at once voluminous and highly characterized by these very difficulties, posing (in addition to the many uncertainties of attribution) a high rate of such perplexities.

As has been said above, the pieces are divided into thirteen categories, many of which are defined by the predominance of techniques, or constellations of techniques, which form indices of their art-historical relationships. This is particularly true of sections 1 to 4 (which focus successively on stone settings, hardstone inlays, hammered precious-metal relief, and engraving on the backs of jewelry items) and of sections 6 and 7 (enamelling and gold-embellished steel, respectively). Section 5 follows a particular application of the techniques of engraving and chiselling expanses of gold in between stone settings to assemble a highly important group of early imperial Mughal pieces and related items. An even narrower focus on a particular group of objects is seen in section 12, namely, inscribed royal gemstones, most of which are spinels. By way of contrast, section 8 is formed of pieces of a variety of types and materials which are distinguished for their three-dimensional sculptural qualities; and those of section 9 were chosen to represent relief carving. Thus, for example, these last two will both be seen to include jade vessels, sometimes involving the separation of generally similar pieces into different groups. Likewise, sections 9 and 11 (the latter concentrating on gemstone forms) both include carved emeralds. Pieces which feature individually carved set gemstones comprise section 10; and while gem-set gold and gold-encrusted objects are scattered through most of the sections, this is the special emphasis in section 13. It seems inevitable that there will be cases in which the choice of grouping may be questioned, but it is confidently believed that the material presented will itself transcend any such problem.

PROBLEMS OF THE HISTORY OF JEWELRY IN THE INDIAN SUBCONTINENT

The character of the present collection affords, among other benefits, an exceptionally instructive index of current knowledge of the history of the jewelry arts in the Subcontinent, and its presentation here will be seen to be equally revealing in this respect.

Despite the unparalleled and (relatively speaking) highly comprehensive nature of this collection, most questions of detail regarding the varieties of Indian jewelry of practically all periods before the Mughal era remain unresolved; and this enormous lacuna prevails particularly in the immediately preceding periods.

The al-Sabah Collection does, however, promote the hope that, just as it has been possible to recognize and secure (and finally present) a number of previously unknown and unsuspected types of the Mughal period, it will be possible to make continuing progress in the recognition and isolation of further as yet unknown types. Thus, it is overwhelmingly likely that, as time goes on, someone will demonstrate the correct placement for various Sultanate-period jewelry types, as well as for those of, for example, the Vijayanagara empire (14th–17th centuries in South India) and of other historical epochs and regions.

Of course, a number of isolated contexts and types of Indian jewelry which predate the Mughal period are known, going back to before the time of Christ. But, in a general sense, these are largely isolated by more than time and space: up to the present,

it is difficult to connect them with each other in any way that will clarify matters for anyone seriously seeking a meaningful chain of transmission. Thus, for all that anyone knows factually, much that characterizes the kind of jewelry represented here – so highly developed and sophisticated, so distinctively and uniquely Indian – seems almost to spring forth from thin air.

It is absolutely clear, however, that as far back in history as any information is available, the art of jewelry has been uniquely prevalent, developed and elaborate in the Indian Subcontinent. Apart from the literary accounts that attest this state of affairs, it is especially the representations in other arts (primarily sculpture and painting) which provide most of the concrete evidence. Any person who has looked at Indian sculpture, for example, will have been struck by the impression that many persons and deities are represented as wearing *only* jewelry. These can, in some cases, give a reasonably good idea of some of the techniques involved, such as repoussé work or certain types of stone cutting, and it is sometimes even possible to identify representations with known extant types.

This said, however, it must be reiterated that, aside from certain generalities, it is seldom possible to connect periods and technical and artistic evolution in any firm manner, and that the need to provide contexts for ancient and medieval pieces, or proper backgrounds for those of the 16th and subsequent centuries, goes largely unfulfilled.

In such circumstances, and in the absence of any large and comprehensive collections of material which would allow detailed comparisons of features to be made, those who have needed to assign dates to objects of the Mughal era have of necessity relied upon a combination of their knowledge of other more securely placed arts of the period and of the relevant history and literature, all usually supplemented with various surmises. Many, in the apparent interests of being 'scientific', have, lacking any absolutely clear indications in the form of such matters as inscriptions or positive identifications in inventories, tended to opt for highly conservative dating. The impression (unconscious though it may be) also often prevails that the vast and rich territories of the Subcontinent which lay outside

Mughal dominion were, with respect to the production of jewelled art, a vast desert, whereas the true situation was quite to the contrary.

For many specialists, a number of our suggestions for regionalization will seem inadequately supported or even downright foolhardy, and much of our dating questionably early. It is undoubtedly true that some of our more daring attributions could be appropriately argued against: like every other author of books dealing with art-historical material on which much work remains to be done, we have had to make difficult choices; and we have simply felt that following the indications of our considered judgment (or our own surmises) was preferable to 'playing it safe' with 'uncontroversial' attributions, particularly since these latter leave one at least as open to error as the former.

THE VISION BEHIND THE COLLECTION
AND THE EXHIBITION

The formation of this collection has been one of Sheikh Nasser's most persistent preoccupations over the past quarter-century, and it is impossible to overstate the degree to which his activity in this respect has been of a pioneering character. It is also impossible for me to communicate the degree to which, or the varieties of ways in which, my own education and connoisseurship in this area of art have been the result of the privilege of studying this collection and of association with Sheikh Nasser in this context. His eye for beauty, quality and a complex range of features, his prodigious memory and his sense of what is important are, quite simply, astounding. His enthusiasm for contemplating works of art, and for dreaming of those that are yet to come to light, make for a most pleasantly infectious atmosphere. And his humility, down-to-earth humanity and eager readiness at all times to debate points in connection with pieces that are being studied stimulate and foster the best efforts in his fellow enthusiasts.

Finally, it is perhaps too easy to overlook Sheikh Nasser's clear, and clearly vindicated, conviction that jewelry and jewelled objects generally – and those of the Indian Subcontinent quite specifically – are works of art which are to be taken seriously, and their creators respected in the highest degree. Here, as in many another point of view, my long-held attitude converges with his, and constitutes one of the many foundations of the fruitfulness of our association.

For the demonstration of the vision and discrimination with which this collection has been formed, it will perhaps suffice to remind ourselves that it is entirely unparalleled. Even within the great museums, the conviction of the validity and importance of jewelry as art has not grown to the point which would allow those institutions, except very occasionally, to acquire important pieces of Indian jewelled arts. Even in the all-too-rare instances in which a curator is enthusiastic to make such an acquisition, the tendency is for the value of such pieces as art objects within a small circle of collectors (and often also their very intrinsic value) to be such that the curator is unable to convince the board of trustees to grant the funds for such a purchase. This is especially the case when, as is typical, there is competition for those funds from other curators who promote more generally accepted types of works of art, such as paintings and sculptures, or other objects of established status.

Although a small number of the pieces in the al-Sabah Collection are celebrated, and have been included in important exhibitions and publications, the overwhelming preponderance of the material is unpublished and unknown, except for presentation and discussion in certain specialized lectures by the author. Included are scores of entirely unsuspected treasures for the history of jewelry, consisting not only of individual masterpieces, but of series of types as yet unknown to the literature.

It seems likely that the making public of this collection will greatly stimulate scholarly study in the area, and will appropriately raise the profile and level of awareness of this and other Indian arts, as well as of the art of jewelry in general. It will also surely inspire future generations of artists, who will have found stimulation in the accomplishments bequeathed by hundreds of generations of artists of the Subcontinent who poured their diligence, skills, artistic refinement and creativity into objects made of precious materials.

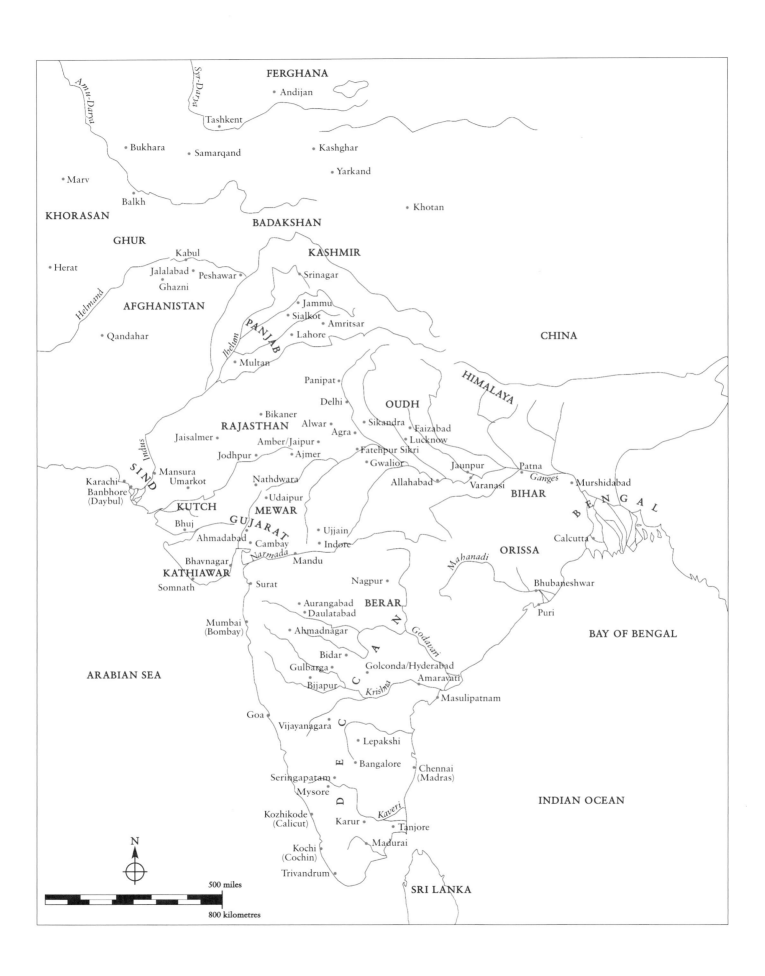

FERGHANA

Andijan

Tashkent

Amu-Darya

Syr-Darya

Bukhara • Samarqand

Kashghar

Marv

Yarkand

Balkh

Khotan

KHORASAN

BADAKSHAN

GHUR

Kabul

KASHMIR

Herat

Jalalabad • Peshawar

Srinagar

Ghazni

Helmand

AFGHANISTAN

Jammu

Sialkot

Amritsar

Qandahar

Jhelum

PANJAB

Lahore

CHINA

Multan

HIMALAYA

Panipat

Delhi

OUDH

Bikaner

Jaisalmer

RAJASTHAN

Alwar

Agra

Sikandra

Faizabad

Lucknow

Amber/Jaipur

Fatehpur Sikri

Jodhpur

Ajmer

Gwalior

Jaunpur

Patna

Allahabad

Varanasi

Ganges

Murshidabad

Indus

SIND

Mansura

Umarkot

Nathdwara

BIHAR

Karachi

Banbhore

(Daybul)

KUTCH

Udaipur

MEWAR

BENGAL

Bhuj

GUJARAT

Ujjain

Calcutta

Ahmadabad

Cambay

Indore

ORISSA

Bhavnagar

Narmada

Mandu

Mahanadi

KATHIAWAR

Somnath

Surat

Nagpur

Bhubaneshwar

Puri

Aurangabad

BERAR

Daulatabad

D E C C A N

Mumbai

(Bombay)

Ahmadnagar

Godavari

BAY OF BENGAL

Bidar

Golconda/Hyderabad

Gulbarga

Amaravati

ARABIAN SEA

Bijapur

Krishna

Masulipatnam

Goa

Vijayanagara

Lepakshi

Bangalore

Chennai

(Madras)

Seringapatam

INDIAN OCEAN

Mysore

Kaveri

Kozhikode

(Calicut)

Karur

Tanjore

Kochi

(Cochin)

Madurai

Trivandrum

SRI LANKA

N

500 miles

800 kilometres

HISTORICAL NOTE

Already in the 8th century AD, a lasting Arab/Islamic presence was established in Sind (lower Indus region) and, from that time on, a number of little-known but thriving Islamic principalities, ruling from major cities, not only held out but flourished there and in Multan, further up the Indus. Excavations at the port of Daybul and at Mansura in Multan have revealed ample testimony to the forging of the earliest of many Islamic syntheses on the soil of the Subcontinent, including remarkable material which shows the adaptability on both sides of the equation – traditional Islamic and traditional Indian – and the originality and creativity of artists in the region in adjusting to new influences, creating new styles and expanding horizons.

Thus, the conquests and yearly deep raids from Afghanistan of Mahmud of Ghazni (first third of the 11th century) and the establishment in the later 11th and 12th centuries of a Ghaznavid capital and highly cultivated centre at Lahore are to be seen as part of a general and long-term encroachment of Islamic power and culture into the Subcontinent. By the late 12th and early 13th century, the Ghurids (who were the Ghaznavids' successors as the power in Afghanistan and the Panjab) and their military commanders who were left behind were able to establish their rule over much of northern India, including Delhi itself.

Thenceforward, a series of dynasties of Turkic and Afghan origin ruled from Delhi over generally increasing territories, although from the 14th century various of them (most notably in the Deccan) broke away from the Sultanate in Delhi to become independent. It was the Delhi Sultanate, ruled at the time by the Lodi dynasty, which was conquered in 1526 by the prince Babur, who established himself as the first 'Mughal' emperor. Babur was born in Central Asia, a descendant of Timur (known in the West as Tamerlane) and Genghis Khan. His son and successor, Humayun, after a ten-year reign, was driven out by Shir Shah Sur (leader of the Afghan commanders in northern India), whose line ruled for fifteen years. Humayun was, however, able in 1555 to return from his exile in Iran and re-establish himself at Delhi, after which the Mughals' rule lasted officially until the last emperor, Bahadur Shah, was deposed by the British in 1857.

It was particularly in the reigns of Humayun's son, Akbar, and his two successors, Jahangir and Shah Jahan, that a hundred-year-long period of might and glory (1556–1657) established the everlasting fame of the 'Great Moguls'. They were fabled in the West at the time, and no richer or more distinguished connoisseurs have drawn breath; however, they should not be seen in isolation, but as part of a general and ages-long pattern in the Subcontinent, which had been the fabulously wealthy East since the time of the Greeks and Romans.

In the Deccan, a great Muslim-ruled dominion, the Bahmanid kingdom, had developed from about the mid-14th century, eventually reaching from the eastern to the western coasts; but by the late 15th century it too broke up into five major kingdoms: the 'Imad Shahis, ruling from Berar; the Barid Shahis, ruling from Bidar; the 'Adil Shahis, ruling from Bijapur; the Nizam Shahis, ruling from Ahmadnagar; and the Qutb Shahis, ruling from Golconda/Hyderabad. These kingdoms went through various processes of elimination until the last of them, those of the 'Adil Shahis of Bijapur and of the Qutb Shahis of Golconda/Hyderabad, came under the sway, and eventually the outright rule (1686 and 1687, respectively), of the Mughals.

Aside from the Hindu kingdoms of the southern part of India (most notably Vijayanagara), an additional centre of power, wealth and influence, from the early 16th century, was the Portuguese enclave of Goa, which was one of the main gates for trade and artistic exchanges in the earlier part of the period represented in this catalogue and exhibition.

India was blessed as the only significant source of diamonds before their discovery in Brazil in the 18th century, and she was also made rich by her spices; but more than any other resource, it was her art industries (most especially textiles, but also including a whole array of specialized and sophisticated products) which she traded for the gold and silver that poured in by the ton. This talent and tradition for fine and artistic craftsmanship, coupled with a wealthy and active class of patrons, is responsible for the marvels which we are privileged to study and now to present to the wider public.

1
VARIETIES IN STONE SETTINGS

Before the beginning of recorded history, mankind was setting contrasting ornamental stones into artistic objects. All the earliest phases of this practice involved cementing such stones into depressions or cells which had been prepared for the purpose, whether the substrate was of precious metal, a separate stone, wood or some other material.

During the first millennium BC, however, a whole series of more secure and elegant, ingenious 'mechanical', systems for holding the inset elements was perfected. Leaving aside the simple collet setting, the more advanced of these may be generally characterized as different varieties of highly sophisticated 'hammered' settings, which involved the locking of inlays into place by the physical displacement of metal inwards and over their edges.

It appears that these developments overwhelmingly took place in the steppelands of Eurasia, whence they spread outwards in cultural streams of varying strength in different directions and at different rates of movement. Among these hammered setting types was the 'gipsy' setting, still practised to a limited extent today, in which an isolated stone is placed in an excavated cavity, the surrounding metal then being displaced laterally by blows, typically administered by means of a smooth, round-ended punch.

Another Eurasian heritage of the first millennium BC is what we may call the 'hammered-cloison' setting, which, as practised in European objects during the 'Tribal Migrations' and early medieval periods, is reasonably widely known. This type seems to have existed in fully developed form in the Steppes during the first half of the first millennium BC, thence to reach and be practised in India, Iran and Europe in the early centuries of the new era; it was manifest at a particularly high level in Europe, before dying out around the end of the third quarter of the millennium.

While producing extremely rich effects (particularly as a result of the ability to cover entire surfaces of objects with gemstones), the hammered-cloison setting was inordinately labour-intensive because of the need for a high degree of control of design and execution, including the thickness of stones, the height of cloisons and the fit of the two in plan. In Europe it gave way to simpler techniques, especially the collet setting, in which the upper edge of a simple, edge-set, strip-constructed metal ring is forced in and over the perimeter of the stone. Variants of the collet setting were also popular, often in the form of beautifully decorative rosettes provided with claws. These had the advantage of ease in the setting process as well as allowing the display of a larger proportion of the stone, while still holding it securely.

Unfortunately, collet settings of whatever kind cannot be grouped closely enough together to give real freedom to the artist in making patterns with stones. It is surely from the desire to achieve such design freedom, and against the backdrop of the practice of hammered-cloison setting, that the jewelry artists of India, probably in the centuries immediately preceding the birth of Christ, developed their unique treasure, the *kundan* setting.

Kundan, or hyper-purified gold, is beaten into narrow strips of foil and refined to the point at which it becomes 'tacky' at room temperature. At this degree of purity, it can actually form a molecular bond when pressure is applied to it by means of steel tools, which are first used to press the foil down around the stones, then to cut, shape and burnish it into any form that the artist may wish. *Kundan* can be applied over any rigid surface, and since there is no need for soldering to join the metal, it bestows almost complete freedom, whether the work is executed in conjunction with enamels or with previously set stones, or even with organic materials such as wood and ivory. There is no indication that this technique was ever practised anywhere except in India, despite its obvious advantages, and despite the fact that its visual effect was much imitated in the surrounding regions.

1.1

1.2

1.2   FINGER RING
LNS 342 J

Fabricated from gold; worked in *kundan* technique
    and set with a ruby and natural diamond crystals
Height 28 mm; width 29 mm
India, perhaps Deccan, late 16th–earlier 17th century AD
Art market, 1994

1.1   SMALL BOTTLE
LNS 959 J

Fabricated from gold; worked in *kundan* technique and
    set with rubies, emeralds and natural diamond crystals
Height including cap 46 mm; width 40 mm; thickness 17 mm
Probably northern India, *c.* 1st third 17th century AD
Art market, 1993

1.3

1.3   FINGER RING
LNS 1170 J

Fabricated from gold; worked in *kundan* technique and set
    with rubies, turquoises and natural diamond crystals
Height 28 mm; width 22 mm
India, perhaps Deccan, late 16th–earlier 17th century AD
Art market, 1994

1.4 SWORD HILT, LOCKET AND CHAPE
LNS 2158 Ja–c

The hilt gold over an iron core, ringmatted;
   the locket and chape fabricated from gold;
   all worked in *kundan* technique and set with rubies,
   emeralds and (the hilt and chape with) diamonds
Length of hilt excluding bail 182 mm; width at quillons 89 mm;
   diameter of disc 61 mm; length of locket 66 mm;
   width including lug 55 mm; thickness 19 mm;
   length of chape 145 mm; width 42 mm
India, probably Mughal, perhaps last quarter
   16th–earlier 17th century AD
Art market, 1999

1.5

1.5 PENDANT OF *TAVIZ* (AMULET) TYPE
LNS 2200 J

Fabricated from gold; worked in *kundan* technique
   and set with rubies, diamonds and emeralds
Height 24 mm; length 45 mm; thickness 19 mm
India, probably Mughal, probably earlier 17th century AD
Art market, 1999

1.4

1.6 PAIR OF BRACELETS
LNS 168 Ja, b

Fabricated from gold sheet
    (probably filled with lac);
    worked in *kundan* technique
    and set with rubies and diamonds
Average max. diameter 77 mm;
    average max. width
    excluding clasp screw 17 mm
India, probably Mughal,
    probably 17th century AD
Art market, 1978

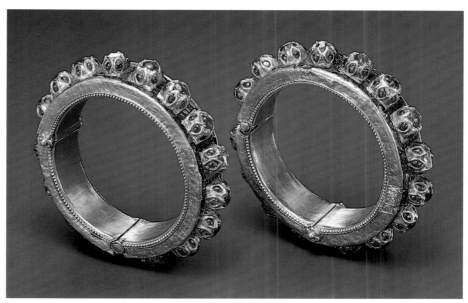

1.6

1.7 PAIR OF EARPLUGS
LNS 1809 Ja, b

Fabricated from gold; worked in
    kundan technique and set with
    rubies, diamonds and emeralds;
    and with pearls and tiny ruby
    beads pendant on gold wires
Average height 82 mm;
    average width 63 mm;
    average diameter of discs 43 mm
India, probably Mughal,
    probably earlier 17th century AD
Art market, 1997

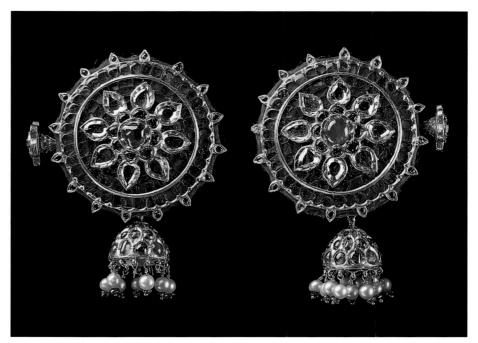

1.7

1.8   TINY BOX
LNS 1803 J

Fabricated from gold; worked in *kundan* technique
    and set with rubies
Height 23 mm; length 29 mm;
    width excluding hinge and hasp 26 mm
Western India, Deccan or Mughal, probably 17th century AD
Art market, 1997

1.8

1.9   UPPER ARMBAND (*BĀZŪBAND*)
LNS 753 J

Fabricated from gold; worked in *kundan* technique
    and set with banded agates and diamonds
Length 89 mm; width 41 mm
India, Deccan or Mughal, 17th century AD
Art market, 1993

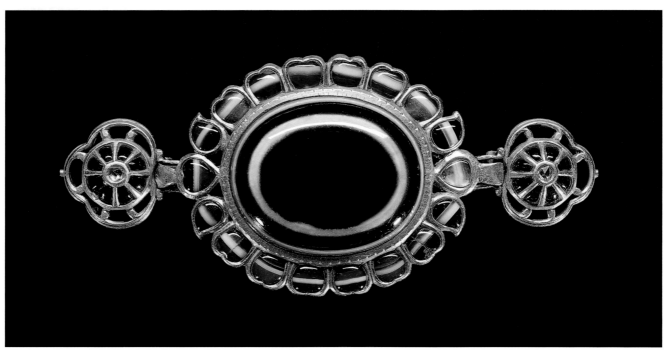

1.9

1.10   PENDANT OF *TAVIZ* (AMULET) FORM
LNS 1161 J

Fabricated from gold; worked in *kundan* technique
    and set with rubies
Height 19 mm; length 28 mm; thickness 13 mm
India, Deccan or Mughal, probably 1st half 17th century AD
Art market, 1994

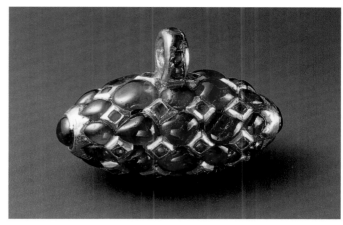

1.10

1.11

1.11   PENDANT
LNS 2198 J

Plaque of grey nephrite jade; inlaid with gold in *kundan*
    technique and set with rubies and emeralds; the back
    and loops fabricated from gold with champlevé enamels;
    with pendant spinel bead
Overall height 56 mm; height excluding gold bail
    and pendant spinel 33 mm; width 29 mm; thickness 6 mm
Jade plaque India, probably Deccan, probably 1st quarter
    17th century AD; frame and back India, probably Deccan,
    later 18th–19th century AD
Art market, 1999

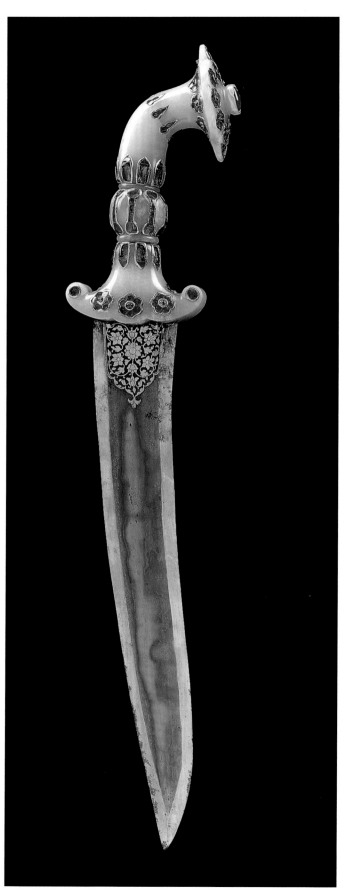

1.12   DAGGER
LNS 2221 J

Blade of *jawhar* steel, overlaid with gold of two colours;
    hilt of nephrite jade (white, with subtle cloudlike areas of
    lower translucency), inlaid with gold and set with rubies
    and emeralds in *kundan* technique
Length 395 mm; max. width 93 mm
India, probably Deccan, 1st half 17th century AD
Art market, 1999
Published: Habsburg, Feldman, Geneva, 29 June 1988, lot 294;
    Christie's, London, 6 October 1999, 2, lot 198

1.13   JEWELLED MOUNT
LNS 1186 J

Plaque of nephrite jade (translucent light greenish grey);
    inlaid with gold in *kundan* technique and set with rubies
    and emeralds
Diameter 46 mm; thickness 7 mm
India, Deccan or Mughal, probably 1st half 17th century AD
Art market, 1994
Published: Sotheby's, New York, 7 June 1994, lot 93

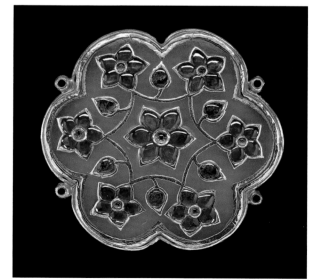

1.12   1.13

1.14   FINGER RING
LNS 769 J

Fabricated from gold, worked in repoussé and in *kundan* technique
    and set with rubies and emeralds
Height 33 mm; bezel diameter 26 mm
India, Deccan or Mughal, 17th century AD
Art market, 1993

1.14

1.15   FINGER RING
LNS 1862 J

Fabricated from gold; worked in *kundan* technique
    and set with rubies and an emerald; shank engraved
Height 35 mm; bezel diameter 30 mm
India, probably Deccan, probably 17th century AD
Art market, 1997
Published: Christie's, South Kensington, 7 October 1997, lot 744

1.16

1.15

1.16   JEWELRY ELEMENT
LNS 1816 J

Fabricated from gold; worked in *kundan* technique
    and set with rubies, emeralds, diamonds and pearls
Height 45 mm; width 44 mm; thickness 7 mm
India, Mughal or Deccan, 1st half 17th century AD
Art market, 1997

1.17

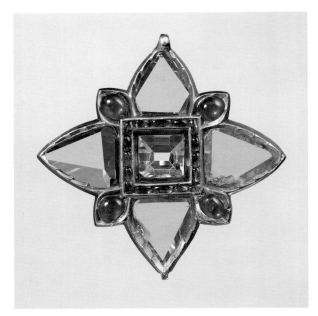

1.18

1.18 PENDANT
LNS 341 J

Fabricated from gold; worked in *kundan* technique
 and set with diamonds (the centre stone cut and polished,
 the petals natural unpolished flats), rubies and emeralds
Height 47 mm; width 45 mm; thickness 4 mm
India, Deccan or Mughal, perhaps 1st quarter 17th century AD
Art market, 1992

1.19 PENDANT
LNS 1212 J

Fabricated from gold; worked in *kundan* technique
 and set with diamonds, rubies and emeralds;
 with pendant emerald bead
Height excluding pendant emerald 46 mm;
 height including pendant emerald 64 mm;
 width 39 mm; thickness excluding pendant emerald 8 mm
India, Deccan or Mughal, 1st half 17th century AD
Art market, 1995

1.17 FOREHEAD ORNAMENT
LNS 2008 J

Fabricated from gold; worked in *kundan* technique
 and set with rubies, emeralds and diamonds;
 strung with pearls and with pendant ruby bead and pearls
Height excluding hook 99 mm;
 width excluding pendant elements 22 mm;
 thickness excluding pendant elements 3 mm
India, Mughal or Deccan, probably 17th century AD
Art market, 1998

1.20 PENDANT
LNS 955 J

Fabricated from gold; worked in *kundan* technique
 and set with diamonds, rubies and emeralds;
 with pendant pearl and enamelled cap
Height excluding pendant pearl 36 mm;
 height including pendant pearl 52 mm;
 width 30 mm; thickness excluding pendant pearl 6 mm
India, Deccan or Mughal, probably 1st half 17th century AD
Art market, 1993

1.19

1.20

1.21

1.21 PENDANT
LNS 1210 J
Fabricated from gold; worked in *kundan* technique
    and set with diamonds, rubies and emeralds;
    with pendant emerald bead
Height excluding pendant emerald 50 mm;
    height including pendant emerald 67 mm;
    width 39 mm; thickness excluding pendant emerald 9 mm
India, Deccan or Mughal, probably 1st half 17th century AD
Art market, 1995

1.22

1.22   PENDANT
LNS 1211 J
Fabricated from gold; worked in *kundan* technique
     and set with diamonds and rubies; with pendant pearl
Height excluding pendant pearl 36 mm;
      height including pendant pearl 48 mm;
      width 27 mm; thickness excluding pendant pearl 6 mm
India, Deccan or Mughal, probably 1st half 17th century AD
Art market, 1995

1.23   TURBAN ORNAMENT
LNS 1767 J
Fabricated from gold; with champlevé and overpainted enamels;
      worked in *kundan* technique and set with emeralds
      and diamonds
Height 173 mm; width 53 mm;
      thickness including plume holder 13 mm
India, probably Deccan (Hyderabad?),
      probably 2nd half 17th century AD
Art market, 1997

1.23

1.24

1.25

1.24   PENDANT
LNS 1176 J
Fabricated from gold; worked in *kundan* technique and set
    with emeralds and rubies; with pendant emerald bead
Height excluding pendant emerald 39 mm;
    height including pendant emerald 55 mm;
    width 27 mm; thickness excluding pendant emerald 4 mm
India, probably Deccan, probably 1st half 17th century AD
Art market, 1994

1.25   PENDANT
LNS 1141 J
Fabricated from gold, champlevé enamelled;
    worked in *kundan* technique and set with emeralds;
    with pendant emerald bead and enamelled cap
Height excluding pendant emerald 30 mm;
    height including pendant emerald 43 mm;
    width 25 mm; thickness excluding pendant emerald 5 mm
India, probably Deccan, perhaps 17th century AD
Art market, 1994

2

INLAID HARDSTONES

MAN'S EARLIEST ESSAYS in the inlaying of objects made of ornamental stones and analogous materials may also very possibly have constituted the very first attempts at the setting of stones in general (see page 18); certainly, both stemmed from one and the same impulse.

But while the main history of the kind of material grouped under 'Varieties in Stone Settings' was played out in conjunction with precious metal as the substrate, we focus here on the development of specialized techniques and artistic types in which precious metal is locked mechanically into hardstones (and to some extent other materials, such as ivory). In the ultimate development of this discipline – that which typifies the Mughal period in India – the inlaid precious metal is set with the finest of precious stones, creating a dazzling effect, although one which, in the classic phase of the later 16th and 17th centuries, always remained subject to the taste and artistic control of practitioners deeply schooled in a rich and rigorous tradition.

The earliest-known example of precious-metal inlay in hardstones, properly defined, is attributable to the 12th century in the eastern Iranian world. It is tempting to think that this truly represents the earliest phase of the art, and that it has a connection, at some level, with the rise at just this time and in the same region of a great and influential school of copper-alloy metalwork which is inlaid with silver and copper.

The next examples of hardstone inlay which are known at this point date from the 15th century; these were executed in the same region as the 12th-century work, and comparisons of the methods employed show clearly that the same school of work continued over the intervening period. In keeping with earlier precedent, this 15th-century (Timurid period) Iranian school seems predominantly to have taken the form of half-palmette arabesque designs in gold, without any inset stones; the inlay was, however, invariably enlivened by artistically engraved and chiselled interior details of a foliate character.

At least occasionally it also included stones, which were set by a method in which metal is scarped inward with a graver and pushed over the edge of the stone, similar to the procedure of modern 'bead' settings, most often used for 'pavé' schemes.

This Timurid school of inlay continued under the Safavids in the early 16th century, the tradition also being inherited by the Ottoman Turks, most likely as a result of their capture of the Safavid capital of Tabriz (where they acquired rich booty and numerous craftsmen) in 1514.

Despite several centuries of development in Iran, the difficulties inherent in the inlaying of hardstones (and the like) with massive metal, however pure, limited the freedom of the artist and the range of effective and aesthetically pleasing types of inlay that were possible. These limitations, together with some unfortunate results of attempts to expand the range of types, are most apparent in the extensive Ottoman Turkish material. In this body of work, the problems are particularly obvious in examples set with stones (as distinct from another Ottoman type of inlay in which only flush-inlaid, plain gold is incorporated), where the inlays give the effect of being at uncomfortable odds with the objects they are intended to adorn.

In India, it was once again a case of the ideal technique, *kundan* (see page 18), being available; and it was because of the *kundan* technique that the gold of the inlayer, or *zar-nishān* was (as the emperor Akbar's minister and historian Abu 'l-Fazl put it) 'made so pure and ductile that the fable of the gold of Parviz which he could mould with his hand becomes credible'. Thus, the inlayer could cut his grooves as he wished and put as much or as little gold whenever and wherever he wanted, and set it with as many or as few stones as required; he was free to make his pieces as much a delight to see and to handle as his taste would allow. The pieces which are featured here bear eloquent witness to the fact that this level of taste was very impressive indeed and happily allied with incomparable technical means.

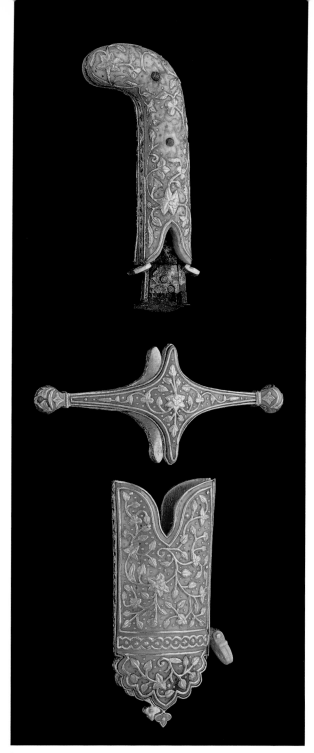

2.1

2.2

2.2 ARCHERY RING
LNS 366 HS
Carved from nephrite jade (white, uniform and translucent,
    of a high degree of purity of colour); inlaid with gold
    in *kundan* technique
Length front to back 40 mm; width 30 mm; height 14 mm
India, Deccan or Mughal, later 16th–early 17th century AD
Art market, 1999
Published: Sotheby's, London, 22 April 1999, 2, lot 279

2.3

2.1 SWORD HILT, QUILLONS AND LOCKET
LNS 97 Ia–c
The facings carved from walrus ivory; inlaid with gold in *kundan*
    technique; the iron strip which runs around the entire edge of
    the hilt covered with a layer of gold and engraved; the backing
    and edges of the quillons and locket fabricated from gold
    and engraved
Length of assembled elements 224 mm;
    width 121 mm; max. thickness 29mm
India, Deccan or Mughal, last quarter 16th century AD
Art market, 1998

2.3 SWORD HILT
LNS 37 I
The grip-slabs carved from walrus ivory; inlaid with gold,
    the latter engraved; the edges of the iron framework
    covered with plain gold
Length 110 mm; width 39 mm;
    max. thickness 25mm (excluding silver rivets)
Probably Deccan, Bijapur, dated AH 1044/AD 1634–35
Art market, 1980s
Published: Keene 1984, no. 39

2.4

2.4   PENDANT INSCRIBED IN THE NAME OF THE EMPEROR SHAH JAHAN
LNS 120 J

Carved from nephrite jade (light, uniform grey, translucent);
    inlaid with gold in *kundan* technique;
    fabricated gold frame and suspension lugs
Height 45 mm; width 38 mm; thickness 6 mm
India, Mughal, dated AH 1047/AD 1637–38
Art market, 1988
Published: Atil 1990, no. 96 (also in the French, Italian, German,
    Portuguese and Arabic editions); Dehejia 1997, fig. 214

2.5   DAGGER HILT, LOCKET AND CHAPE
LNS 256 HSa–c

Carved from rock crystal; inlaid with gold in *kundan* technique
    and set with rubies, emeralds and banded agate
Length of hilt 130 mm; width 70 mm;
    length of locket 33 mm; width 42 mm;
    length of chape 38 mm; width 23 mm
India, Mughal, later 16th–1st decade 17th century AD
    (with later alterations and additions)
Art market, 1997

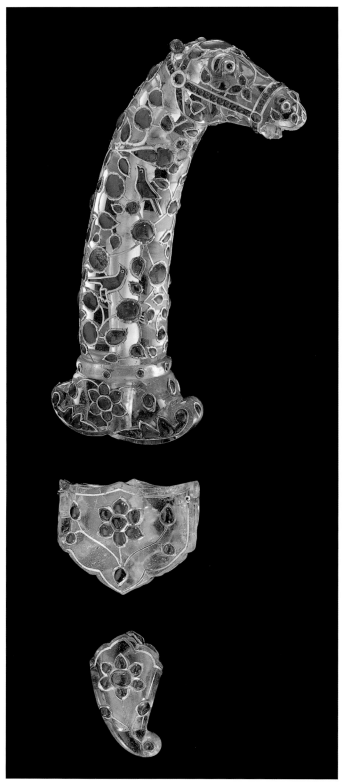

2.5

2.6

2.7

2.6   CUP
LNS 208 HS

Carved from rock crystal; inlaid with gold in *kundan* technique
and set with rubies, emeralds and dark sapphire-blue glass;
the stones underlain (toward the interior) with painted
miniature faces and with kingfisher feathers

Height 48 mm; diameter 85 mm

India, Deccan or Mughal, later 16th–early 17th century AD

Art market, 1994

2.7   CUP
LNS 368 HS

Carved from rock crystal; inlaid with gold in *kundan* technique
and set with rubies and emeralds

Height 53 mm; diameter 70 mm

India, Deccan or Mughal, later 16th–early 17th century AD

Art market, 1999

2.8   HILT
LNS 118 J

Carved from rock crystal; inlaid with gold in *kundan* technique
and set with rubies and emeralds

Length 108 mm; width 63 mm

India, Deccan or Mughal, later 16th–early 17th century AD

Art market, 1980s

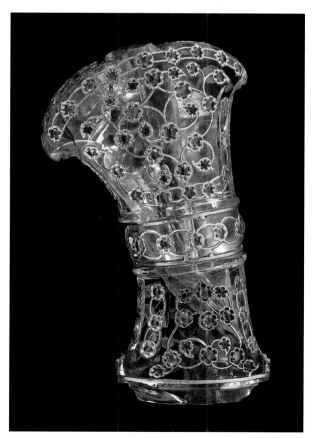

2.8

2.9

2.9 CUP
LNS 140 J

Carved from nephrite jade (dull light greyish green);
  inlaid with gold in *kundan* technique and set with rubies,
  emeralds, turquoise, sapphire and transparent dark
  sapphire-blue and transparent emerald-green glass
Height 32 mm; diameter 57 mm
India, Mughal or Deccan, later 16th–early 17th century AD
Gift to the Collection, 1980s

2.10 CHILD'S DAGGER (?)
LNS 75 HS

Blade of *jawhar* steel (of the broad period but not original
  to this piece); hilt carved from nephrite jade (palest greyish
  off-white), inlaid with gold in *kundan* technique and set with
  rubies, emeralds and a single sapphire; quillons probably iron,
  heavily covered with gold worked in *kundan* technique and
  set with rubies and emeralds
Length 235 mm; width at quillons 46 mm
India, probably Mughal, 1st–2nd decade 17th century AD
Art market, 1991

2.10

2.11

2.11 BOX
LNS 209 HS

Carved from rock crystal; inlaid with gold in *kundan* technique
   and set with rubies and emeralds; the interior fabricated
   from gold and silver
Height 57 mm; diameter 51 mm
India, Deccan or Mughal, later 16th–earlier 17th century AD
Art market, 1994

2.12

2.12 BOX
LNS 369 HS

Carved from nephrite jade (pale grey off-white); inlaid with gold
   in *kundan* technique and set with rubies and emeralds
Height including lid 32 mm;
   max. width (corner to corner) 88 mm
India, probably Deccan, *c.* mid-17th century AD
Art market, 1999

2.13   SPOON
LNS 254 HS

Carved from nephrite jade (pale greenish grey with russet
  areas); inlaid with gold in *kundan* technique and set with
  rubies and emeralds
Length 102 mm; width 31 mm
India, probably Mughal, 1st half 17th century AD
Art market, 1997
Published: Sotheby's, London, 8 May 1997, lot 144

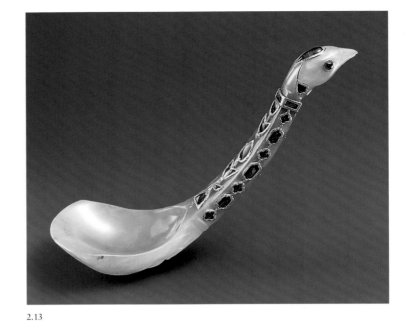

2.13

2.14

2.14   KNIFE
LNS 211 HS

Blade of *jawhar* steel
  overlaid with gold
  (blade and integral
  socket historic and
  Indian, but not
  original to this hilt);
  hilt carved from white
  nephrite jade (bud
  translucent white;
  grip translucent off-
  white with extremely
  subtle mottling), inlaid
  with gold in *kundan*
  technique and set with
  rubies; the gold cap
  champlevé-enamelled
Length 220 mm;
  width 14 mm
India, probably Deccan,
  c. mid-17th century AD
Art market, 1994

2.15   *KATAR* DAGGER AND SCABBARD WITH
ORIGINAL LOCKET AND CHAPE
LNS 68 HS

Blade of *jawhar* steel; hilt, locket and chape of nephrite jade
  (translucent pale grey off-white, with white flecks),
  inlaid with gold in *kundan* technique and set with rubies
  and emeralds; scabbard wood overlaid with green velvet,
  the latter with metal thread trimming
Length 412 mm; width 92 mm; length in scabbard 457 mm
India, Deccan or Mughal, *c.* mid-17th century AD
Art market, 1991

2.16   DAGGER AND SCABBARD
WITH LOCKET AND CHAPE
LNS 12 HS

Blade steel (probably *jawhar*, subsequent polishing having
  obscured the 'watering'); hilt, locket and chape carved from
  nephrite jade (hilt and locket subtly mottled white with
  significant russet areas, chape pale uniform off-white grey);
  inlaid with gold in *kundan* technique and set with rubies,
  emeralds and diamonds; scabbard wood, covered with red
  and gold silk velvet (supplementary weft of gold thread)
Length 354 mm; width 80 mm; length in scabbard 390 mm
India, Deccan or Mughal, *c.* mid-17th century AD
Art market, 1980s
Published: Jenkins, Keene and Bates 1983, p. 129;
  Atil, Chase and Jett 1985, fig. 74; Qaddumi 1987, p. 154;
  Atil 1990, no. 100 (also in the French, Italian and German
  editions)

2.15

2.16

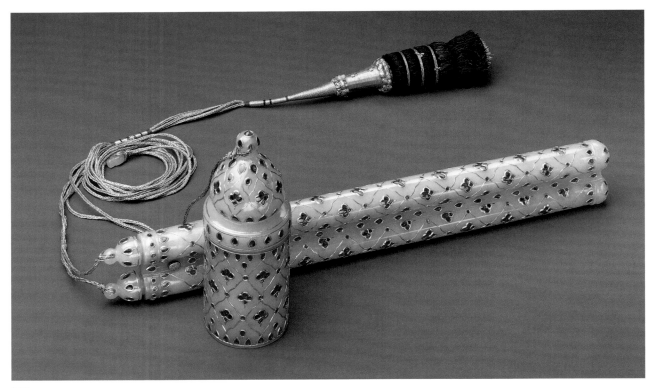

2.17

2.17   INKSTAND
LNS 84 HS

Carved from nephrite jade (pale greenish grey off-white, with extremely subtle variations in
   translucency); inlaid with gold in *kundan* technique and set with rubies and emeralds;
   the inkwell lined with silver
Length 275 mm; width 41 mm; height 110 mm
India, probably Mughal, *c.* mid-17th century AD
Art market, 1991

2.18   FLY-WHISK HANDLE
LNS 210 HS

Carved from nephrite jade (very slightly greenish off-white) bored and 'strung' on an iron rod
   (which affects the colour appearance of the shaft); inlaid with gold in *kundan* technique
   and set with rubies and emeralds
Length including projecting iron rod 210 mm; max. diameter 29 mm
India, Mughal or Deccan, *c.* mid-17th century AD
Art market, 1994

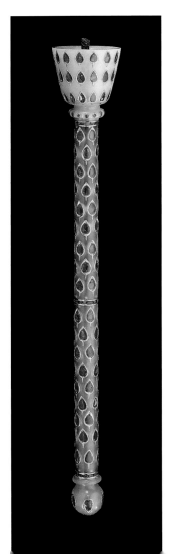

2.18

2.19

2.19 FINGER RING
LNS 180 J

Carved from one piece of dark orange
    cornelian; inlaid with gold in *kundan*
    technique and set with emeralds
    and diamonds
Diameter 26 mm; band width 7 mm
India, probably Mughal,
    probably 17th century AD
Art market, 1991
Published: Sotheby's, London,
    24 and 25 April 1991, lot 723

2.20

2.20 CHAPE FROM A DAGGER SCABBARD
LNS 285 HS

Carved from nephrite jade (pale grey off-white);
    inlaid with gold in *kundan* technique and
    set with rubies and emeralds
Length 55 mm; width 29 mm;
    max. thickness 16mm
India, probably Deccan, *c.* 2nd quarter–mid-17th century AD
Art market, 1997

2.21

2.21 CHAPE FROM A DAGGER SCABBARD
LNS 286 HS

Carved from nephrite jade (pale grey off-white);
    inlaid with gold in *kundan* technique and
    set with rubies, diamonds and emeralds
Length 46 mm; width 22 mm;
    max. thickness 17mm
India, probably Deccan,
    c. 2nd quarter–mid-17th century AD
Art market, 1997

2.22 SOCKET
LNS 53 HS

Carved from nephrite jade
    (translucent white);
    inlaid with gold in
    kundan technique and
    set with rubies and
    emeralds
Length 52 mm;
    max. diameter 10 mm
India, Mughal or Deccan,
    probably 17th century AD
Art market, 1989

2.22

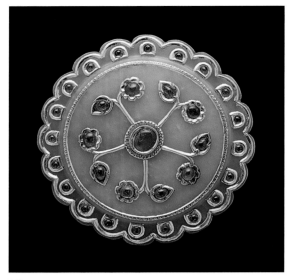

2.23

2.23   HORSE STRAP FITTING
LNS 2101 J

Carved from nephrite jade (pale tan); inlaid with gold
    in *kundan* technique and set with rubies
Diameter 52 mm; thickness 14 mm
India, Mughal or Deccan, 17th century AD
Art market, 1998

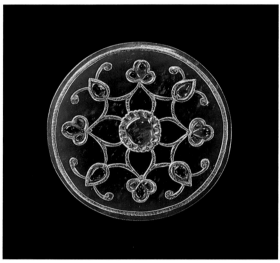

2.25

2.25   DAGGER SASH-CORD ORNAMENT
LNS 1262 J

Carved from nephrite jade (middle green with areas of white
    mottling); inlaid with gold in *kundan* technique and set
    with rubies
Diameter 38 mm; thickness 11 mm
India, Mughal or Deccan, 17th century AD
Art market, 1995

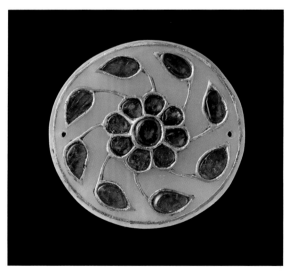

2.24

2.24   DAGGER SASH-CORD ORNAMENT
LNS 259 HS

Carved from nephrite jade (translucent slightly off-white);
    inlaid with gold in *kundan* technique and set with
    rubies and emeralds
Diameter 44 mm; thickness 11 mm
India, Deccan or Mughal, 17th century AD
Art market, 1997

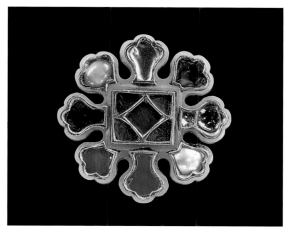

2.27

2.27 DAGGER SASH-CORD ORNAMENT, SET WITH THE NINE AUSPICIOUS GEMS OR *NAVARATNA*
LNS 257 HS

Carved from nephrite jade (pale greyish off-white, with minor areas of whitish and of russet material, yet altogether quite uniform); inlaid with gold in *kundan* technique and set with rubies, diamond, pearl, coral, zircon, blue sapphire, chrysoberyl cat's eye, yellow topaz and emerald
Diameter 35 mm; thickness 12 mm
India, Mughal or Deccan, probably 17th century AD
Art market, 1997

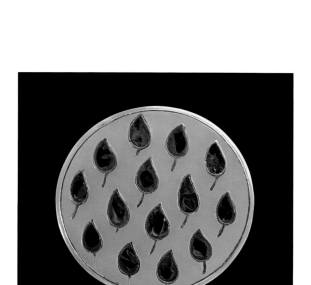

2.26

2.26 DAGGER SASH-CORD ORNAMENT
LNS 212 HS

Carved from nephrite jade (translucent white of great uniformity and very slight greyish cast); inlaid with gold in *kundan* technique and set with rubies
Diameter 42 mm; thickness 14 mm
India, Mughal or Deccan, mid–2nd half 17th century AD
Art market, 1994

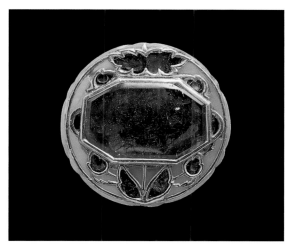

2.28

2.28 DAGGER SASH-CORD ORNAMENT
LNS 258 HS

Carved from nephrite jade (translucent slightly greyish off-white); inlaid with gold in *kundan* technique and set with a spinel and emeralds
Diameter 28 mm; thickness 10 mm
India, Mughal or Deccan, probably 17th century AD
Art market, 1997

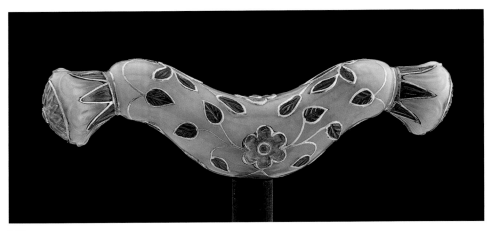

2.29

**2.29 CRUTCH ('*ẒAFAR TAKĪYA*') HEAD
LNS 214 HS**

Carved from nephrite jade (pale greenish grey); inlaid with gold in *kundan*
    technique and set with rubies, rock crystal, lapis lazuli and jade
Height 35 mm; width 120 mm; max. thickness 22 mm
India, probably Deccan, *c.* 3rd quarter 17th century AD
Art market, 1994

2.30

**2.30 BELT BUCKLE
LNS 39 HS**

Carved from one piece of nephrite jade (white with slight
    greyish/greenish cast); inlaid with gold in *kundan*
    technique and set with cornelian and jade
Length 77 mm; width 59 mm; thickness 10 mm
India, Deccan or Mughal,
    probably 2nd half 17th century AD
Art market, 1980s

**2.31 DAGGER AND SCABBARD WITH LOCKET
LNS 69 HS**

Blade of *jawhar* steel; hilt and locket carved from nephrite jade
    (pale green); inlaid with gold in *kundan* technique and set
    with rubies, emeralds and diamonds; scabbard wood overlaid
    with red velvet, with metal thread trimming
Length 397 mm; width 96 mm; length in scabbard 413 mm
India, probably Deccan, *c.* 4th quarter 17th century AD
Art market, 1991

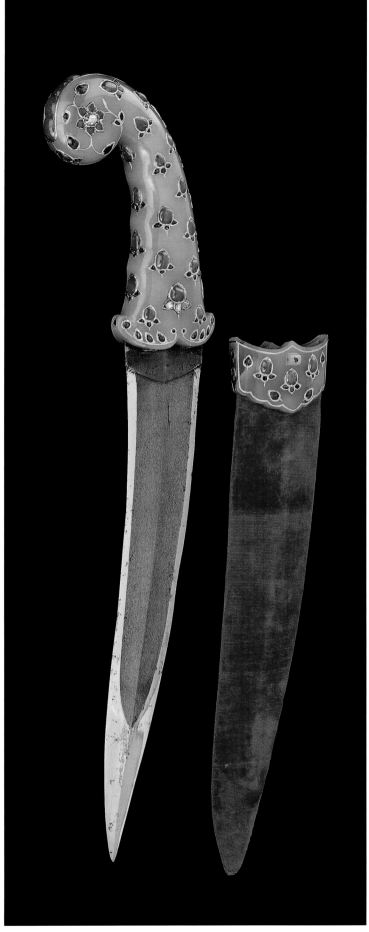

2.31

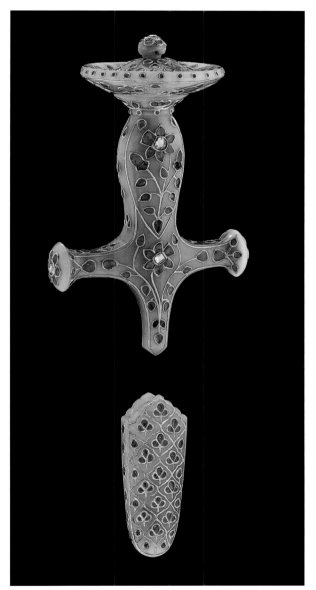

2.32

2.32   SWORD HILT AND CHAPE
LNS 357 HS

Carved from nephrite jade (light greyish green);
   inlaid with gold in *kundan* technique and set
   with rubies, emeralds and diamonds
Length of hilt 168 mm; width of quillons 105 mm;
   diameter of disc 72 mm; length of chape 87 mm;
   width 35 mm
India, Deccan or Mughal, probably later 17th century AD
Art market, 1999

3
RELIEF IN HAMMERED PRECIOUS METAL

LEAVING ASIDE THEIR IMMEDIATE attractiveness of colour and lustre, the most essential characteristic of the noble metals which were discovered and exploited early in the history of civilization is their ability to be hammered (as well as pressed, stretched and drawn) into any form desired, and to hold the shape thus given them. This quality (which copper also shares with silver and gold) is due to these metals' twin properties of malleability and ductility, characteristics which enabled them to reign supreme among non-ferrous metals in use in pre-modern times, and which are still being exploited today to the benefit of mankind.

Long before the beginning of written records, artists were taking advantage of these properties to make objects of gold, and in the early historic phases in Mesopotamia, for example, the 'raising' of tall, elegant vessels of fully controlled shape from sheet gold by hammering the metal over a variety of stakes was thoroughly mastered. Mesopotamian and other early artists also utilized the inherent responsiveness of these metals to produce relief decoration, which was at times so salient from the background as to constitute another 'raised' element of fully three-dimensional character.

Throughout known history, the artists of India have made full use of the responsiveness of such metals, producing truly impressive objects, from enormous vessels and statues to arguably the most minutely detailed repoussé work ever produced, entirely by hammering.

Thus, one could say that it was almost inevitable that the period of prodigious and dynamic artistic efflorescence of the 16th and 17th centuries would give rise to innovations and pinnacles of achievement in decoratively hammered precious metal, as was the case in the other arts. And in hammered work, as in most of those other arts, this age witnessed the introduction of new motifs and approaches from a variety of sources, especially from neighbouring Iran (and through it, in part, ultimately from China) and from Europe.

For various historical reasons, and because of the abundance and high level of patronage in the Subcontinent during this period, India attracted a wide variety of European artists specializing in crafts related to the production of precious-metal and jewelled objects. And in the discipline of hammered precious metals, as in that of enamelling, one can observe the introduction of elements from the repertory of European Renaissance and Baroque design – elements which, in turn, are not infrequently closely analogous to India's own long-standing traditions. This complex confluence is largely due to the shared heritage of classical ornament, which, although still incompletely traced in the Indian context, was nevertheless widespread and pervasive.

Thus, several of the pieces included in this group, while being totally unified products of the artistic consciousness of the maker, present us with particularly striking blends of tradition: in some earlier examples, we can see syntheses which were not maintained into, for instance, the 'middle classic' phase of the Mughal era. And, when studying these early pieces, we can be suddenly struck with rays of insight concerning the background of certain geographically widespread types of Indian hammered-metal work, the resemblances between which were previously baffling.

We may expect that ongoing study will reveal hitherto unrecognized links and seminal stages in the development and spread of the various schools of hammered precious-metal work represented here, from the south to the north and from the west to the east of the Subcontinent. The discovery and definition of such previously unrecognized types and connections are perhaps more likely to come about in relation to the material presented under this heading than with some of the other major disciplines included in this catalogue.

3.1

3.1   BOX
LNS 2192 J
Raised from gold sheet; hammered in relief and chased,
    ground matted with textured chisels
Height 70 mm; diameter 81 mm
India, Deccan or Mughal, later 16th–early 17th century AD
Art market, 1999
Published: Sotheby's, London, 22 April 1999, 1, lot 128

3.2

3.2   WATER-PIPE RESERVOIR (*HUQQA*) AND STAND
LNS 2174 Ja, b
Raised from gold sheet; hammered in relief, chased and punched,
    ground ringmatted, some motifs matted with textured chisels
Height of reservoir 175 mm; diameter 166 mm;
    height of stand 62 mm; diameter of stand 165 mm;
    height of reservoir on stand 207 mm
India, probably Deccan or Western India,
    later 16th–early 17th century AD
Art market, 1999
Published: Habsburg, Feldman, New York, 25 October 1989, lot 182;
    Habsburg, Feldman, Geneva, 14 May 1990, lot 329

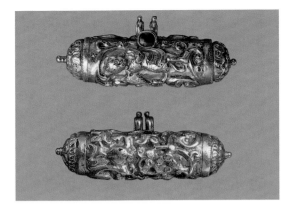

3.4

3.3

3.3   WATER-PIPE RESERVOIR (*HUQQA*)
LNS 1102 M

Raised from silver sheet; hammered in relief, chased and punched,
    ground matted with textured chisels
Height 170 mm; diameter 144 mm
India, Deccan or Mughal, later 16th–early 17th century AD
Art market, 2000

3.4   TWO PENDANTS OF *TAVIZ* (AMULET) FORM
LNS 2245 Ja, b

Fabricated from gold; hammered in relief and chased;
    one set with a garnet
Average height 21 mm; average width 48 mm;
    thickness 15 mm
India, probably Deccan or Western India,
    later 16th–early 17th century AD
Gift to the Collection, 2000

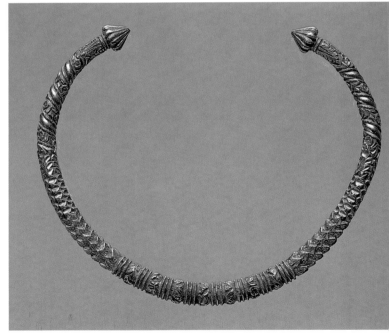

3.5

3.5   TORQUE NECKLACE
LNS 2153 J

Forged from gold, extensively hammered, chiselled and punched
Height back to front 97 mm; width 116 mm
India, probably Deccan or Western India,
    later 16th–early 17th century AD
Art market, 1998

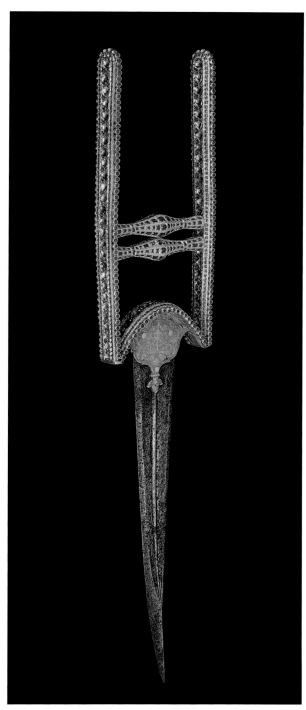

3.6

3.6   *KATAR* DAGGER
LNS 2159 J

Blade steel; hilt gold over an iron core, worked in *kundan*
technique and set with rubies, emeralds and diamonds, and
with settings fabricated from gold sheet; ricasso covered with
a hammered and chased gold sheet plaque, the ground matted
with textured chisels, some motifs matted with 'claw' chisels
Length 432 mm; width 86 mm
India, probably Deccan, 1st third 17th century AD
Art market, 1999

3.7   *KATAR* DAGGER WITH SCABBARD AND CHAPE
LNS 2220 J

Blade steel, pierced through and partially overlaid with gold;
    hilt and chape gold over an iron core, worked in *kundan*
    technique and set with rubies, emeralds and diamonds;
    ricasso covered with a hammered and chased gold sheet plaque,
    the ground ringmatted (as is that of the hilt and the gold-
    overlaid areas of the upper blade); scabbard wood covered
    with purple and gold brocade with metal thread trimmings
Length of dagger 535 mm; width 90 mm;
    length in scabbard 566 mm
India, Deccan or Mughal,
    probably later 16th–1st third 17th century AD
Art market, 1999
Published: Christie's, London, 6 October 1999, 2, lot 197

3.7

3.8

3.8   PENDANT
LNS 2150 J

Fabricated from gold, the front worked in *kundan*
    technique and set with rubies and diamonds;
    the back of gold sheet, hammered and chased
Height 49 mm; width 40 mm; thickness 10 mm
India, Deccan or Mughal,
    probably later 16th–1st third 17th century AD
Art market, 1998

3.9   STRAP FITTINGS
LNS 228 Ja–d

Fabricated from gold, the fronts worked in *kundan* technique and set with
    rubies and emeralds; the back of the large element hammered in relief,
    the ground ringmatted
Height of the largest fitting 57 mm; width 53 mm; thickness 18 mm;
    average diameter of rosettes 34 mm; average thickness 6 mm
India, probably Deccan, later 16th–early 17th century AD
Art market, 1991

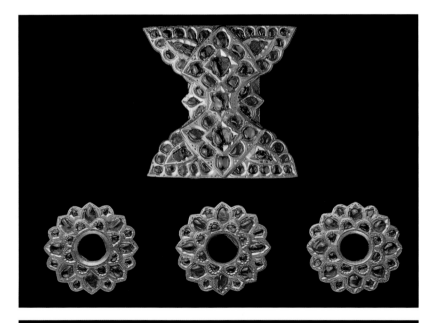

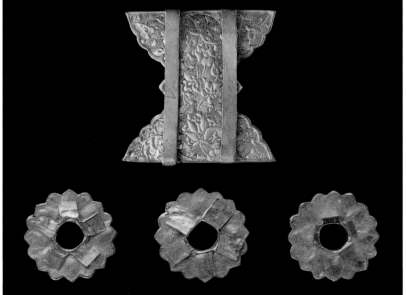

3.9

3.10

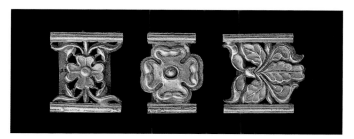

3.12

3.12 STRAP FITTINGS
LNS 1938 Ja–c
Fabricated from silver sheet and strips;
    hammered in relief, cut in openwork and gilded
Average length 24 mm; average width 28 mm;
    average thickness 8 mm
India, probably Mughal, later 16th–earlier 17th century AD
Art market, 1998

3.10 FITTING
LNS 1207 J
Fabricated from gold sheet and twisted wire;
    hammered in relief and chased, the ground ringmatted
Diameter 40 mm; thickness 13 mm
India, probably Mughal, early 17th century AD
Art market, 1994
Published: Christie's, London, 18 and 20 October 1994, lot 373

3.11

3.11 FITTINGS
LNS 1158 Ja–c
Fabricated from silver sheet and strips;
    hammered in relief and gilded
Average diameter 38 mm; average thickness 26 mm
India, probably Mughal, later 16th–early 17th century AD
Art market, 1994

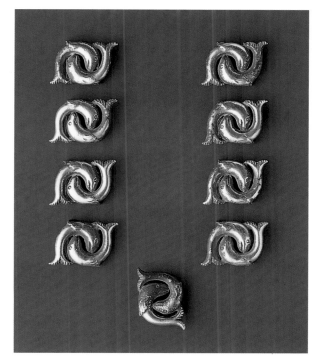

3.13

3.13 STRAP FITTINGS
LNS 2228 Ja–i
Fabricated from silver sheet and strips; matrix-stamped
    and with tool-punched details; cut in openwork
Average height 20 mm; average width 28 mm;
    average thickness 8 mm
India, Deccan or Mughal, later 16th–1st half 17th century AD
Art market, 1999
Published: Bonhams, 13 and 14 October 1999, lot 322

4

ENGRAVED GOLD-BACKED JEWELS

ONE OF THE MOST WIDELY renowned features of Indian jewelry is the elaborate and lovely decoration often lavished on the reverse sides of pieces. There seems, in fact, to be a general perception that such pieces are almost invariably decorated on the back, and that this decoration is virtually always in the form of enamelling.

There is no denying that there is a germ of truth in these impressions; however, as will be seen (especially in the case of items dating from earlier in the period under discussion), there is a considerable variety of treatment of the backs of gem-set jewelled objects. One broad type of reverse decoration, featuring elegant engraving of the gold sheet of the back, is represented by the pieces grouped under this heading.

Features of the engraved decoration itself, as well as other features of the pieces on which the engraved backs occur, allow us to relate them with reasonable reliability to other comparable jewelled material. It is also frequently possible to demonstrate affinities with different artistic manifestations, most notably with architecture, but also with additional types of portable objects of the period. It will be seen that these affinities and relationships, like those of pieces in most of the other categories in this catalogue, tell a story of the blending and assimilation of traditions from a wide range of sources both internal and external to the Subcontinent, to be drawn upon in a seamless process of creation which appears, in the case of the jewelled arts of India, to be endlessly fertile.

4.1

4.1   PENDANT
LNS 954 J

Fabricated from gold, the front worked in *kundan* technique
   and set with rubies, diamonds and emeralds;
    the back gold sheet, engraved; with pendant pearl

Height excluding pendant pearl 38 mm;
   height including pendant pearl 50 mm;
    width 32 mm; thickness 6 mm

India, probably Mughal, *c.* 1st quarter 17th century AD

Art market, 1993

4.2   PENDANT
LNS 1131 J

Fabricated from gold, the front worked in *kundan* technique and
   set with rubies and diamonds; the back gold sheet, engraved;
    with pendant pearl

Height excluding pendant pearl 38 mm;
   height including pendant pearl 49 mm;
    width 34 mm; thickness 4 mm

India, Mughal or Deccan, *c.* 1st half 17th century AD

Art market, 1994

4.2

4.3

4.3 PENDANT
LNS 957 J

Fabricated from gold, the front worked in *kundan* technique
   and set with rubies, diamonds and emeralds;
   the back gold sheet, engraved; with pendant pearl
Height excluding pendant pearl 29 mm;
   height including pendant pearl 40 mm;
   width 24 mm; thickness 7 mm
India, Mughal or Deccan, *c.* 1st half 17th century AD
Art market, 1993

4.4 PENDANT
LNS 1130 J

Fabricated from gold, the front worked in *kundan* technique
   and set with rubies, diamonds and emeralds;
   the back sheet, engraved; with pendant pearl
Height excluding pendant pearl 30 mm;
   height including pendant pearl 41 mm;
   width 23 mm; thickness 5 mm
India, Mughal or Deccan, *c.* 1st half 17th century AD
Art market, 1994

4.4

4.5 PENDANT
LNS 2218 J

Fabricated from gold, the upper surface worked in *kundan*
    technique and set with rubies and diamonds;
      the structure of sheet, engraved; the feet with threaded pearls
Height 32 mm; width 26 mm; thickness 8 mm
India, Mughal or Deccan, *c*. 1st half 17th century AD
Art market, 1999
Published: Christie's, London, 6 October 1999, 2, lot 126

4.5

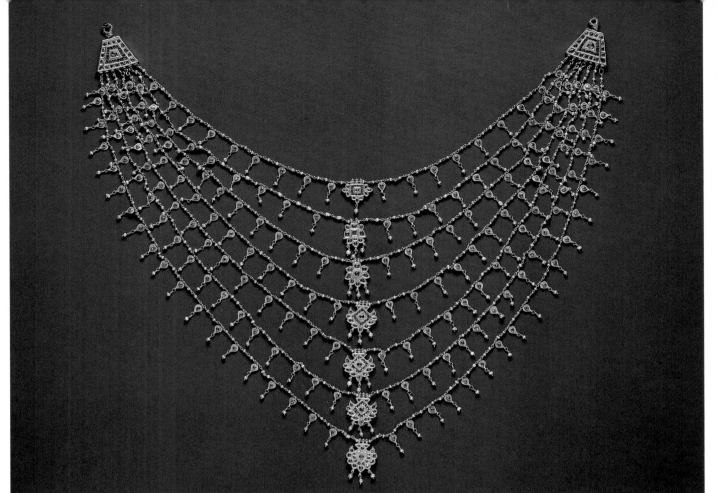

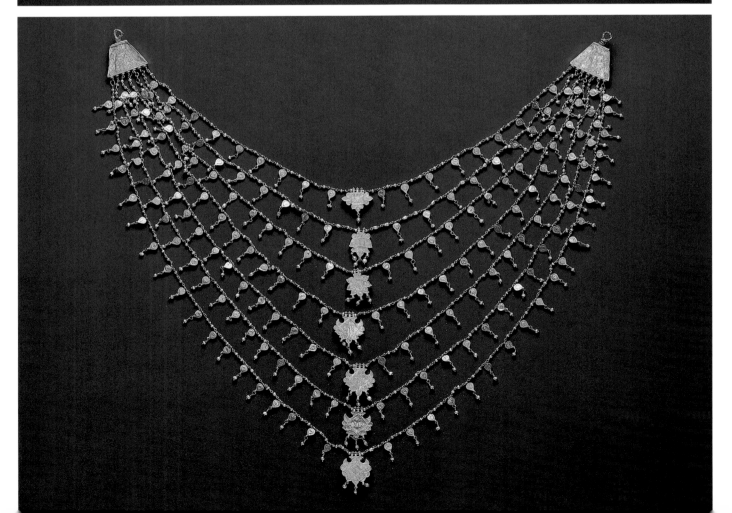

4.6 SEVEN-STRAND NECKLACE
LNS 2170 J

Fabricated from gold, the fronts worked in *kundan*
    technique and set with rubies and emeralds;
    the backs, engraved; strung with pearls
Height 345 mm; width 440 mm
India, Mughal or Deccan, *c*. 1st half 17th century AD
Art market, 1999

4.7 TURBAN ORNAMENT
LNS 2155 Ja, b

Fabricated from gold, the front worked in *kundan*
    technique and set with emeralds, rubies and diamonds;
    the back sheet, engraved; with pendant pearls and
    emeralds
Height of assembled piece 170 mm;
    width 113 mm; thickness 22 mm
India, probably Deccan or Western India,
    2nd half 17th century AD
Art market, 1998
Published: Sotheby's, London, 15 October 1998, 1, lot 153

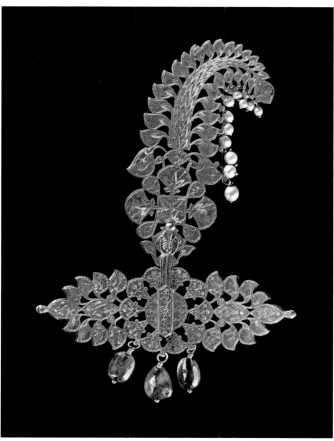

4.7

5

GEMSTONES ON GOLD FLORAL GROUND

Of all the categories into which the material in this catalogue has been divided, this group is the most important in the establishment of the history of the jewelled arts of the period. This is principally because, first, certain key pieces are quite accurately datable and precisely placeable in terms of context or patron; and, second, the group includes a wide range of features which closely parallel those of other types of pieces, helping to place the latter as well as to throw more light on the former.

The single most important feature common to these pieces is the relatively extensive gold ground, which, typically, is engraved and chiselled, the decoration often consisting of quite elaborate floral and foliate motifs, but sometimes also featuring animals and birds in the same style. Although certain ones of the ten pieces grouped here are not in the strictest sense members of the same intimate circle, they have been included on account of relationships which help to define the core group more sharply, and to enable connections with other groups more or less closely related to be made.

The two most important known pieces, in terms of precisely placing the type, are the al-Sabah Collection dagger and scabbard, Cat. no. 5.2 (LNS 25 J), and an archery ring in the State Hermitage Museum in St Petersburg. The first of these is so closely and consistently paralleled by representations in miniature paintings as to leave little doubt that it should be dated to the period around 1610 to 1620, in the reign of the emperor Jahangir (1605–27). The second provides all-important, incontrovertible evidence of origin, since its interior decoration features, on a field of engraved gold that is closely similar to that of the dagger, the title typically used to inscribe objects in the name of Shah Jahan (reigned 1628–58). This beautiful calligraphy is executed in the same kind of sunken, flat, channel-set ruby work as is seen on the above-mentioned dagger, as well as on other members of this tightly related group, including Cat. no. 5.1 (LNS XIX SH).

Because of the intimate similarities between the al-Sabah Collection dagger and Shah Jahan's archery ring, one must place the latter early in his reign; and indeed the entire time-span covering all these very closely related pieces should not, it seems, be more than approximately the working life of one master designer in the royal Mughal workshops. This 'very closely related' group would also include other pieces in the State Hermitage Museum, a wonderful spoon in the Victoria & Albert Museum, London, a beautiful straight dagger and sheath in the Metropolitan Museum of Art, New York, and a dagger in the Wallace Collection, London. This last exhibits a close relationship with Cat. no. 5.2 (LNS 25 J), and is similarly closely paralleled in terms of form and certain intimate features by representations in miniature paintings dating from the period between 1615 and 1620.

The al-Sabah Collection dagger (illustrated opposite) is the most elaborate production of this school known to have survived. It originally included, among other features, more than 2,400 separately cut and set 'stones', of which 2,393 remain, most being rubies, diamonds and emeralds, but also including banded agate, ivory and glass where appropriate. It is extensively engraved, and has a 'repoussé-worked' scabbard back. And yet with all these elements, all this razzle-dazzle, and all the subtle intricacies of design and execution, it is a fully integrated and unified work of art; and one must also emphasize that the delight that it provokes is further enhanced (as with many of the other daggers presented in this catalogue) by the pleasure of physically handling it.

In common with several other members of its group, the incorporation in this dagger of a number of other distinctive and often rare features helps, as suggested above, to place a variety of pieces more closely than might otherwise be possible. These include, for example, the edgings of natural diamond crystals, the specially cut gemstone elements forming corners and edges, certain types of carved precious-stone elements, channel-set lines of precious stones, various decorative motifs and so on, which are precluded by reasons of space from detailed discussion here.

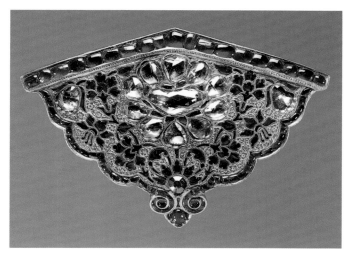

5.1

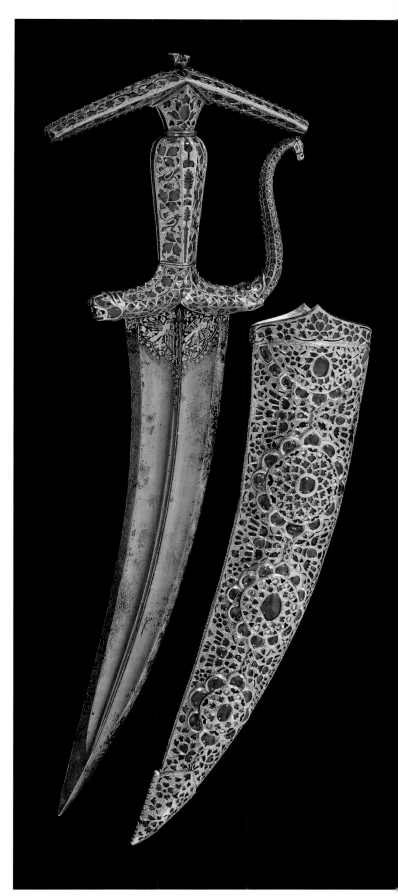

5.1   LOCKET FROM THE SCABBARD OF A
KATAR DAGGER
LNS XIX SH

Fabricated from gold; worked in *kundan* technique, set with
    diamonds, rubies and emeralds, engraved and chiselled
Height 56 mm; width 83 mm
India, Mughal, *c.* 1615–20
Art market, 1980s

5.2   DAGGER AND SCABBARD
LNS 25 J

Blade of *jawhar* steel (later repolished), hatched and overlaid
    with gold; iron hilt, as well as locket, chape and front of
    scabbard, overlaid with gold, worked in *kundan* technique,
    set with precious stones, engraved and chiselled; scabbard
    wood covered on the back with gold sheet hammered in relief;
    hilt and scabbard set with a total of 1,685 rubies, 271 natural
    unpolished diamonds, 62 emeralds, 321 pieces of transparent
    emerald-green glass, 39 pieces of transparent dark middle blue
    glass, 9 pieces of ivory and 6 layered agates (grand total of
    2,393 'stones', to which another 26, now missing, must be
    added, for an original total of 2,419)
Length of dagger 333 mm; length in scabbard 352 mm;
    width 117 mm
India, Mughal, *c.* 1615–20
Art market, 1981
Published: Jenkins, Keene and Bates 1983, p. 126;
    Welch 1985, cat. no. 127; Qaddumi 1987, pp. 121, 153;
    Amsterdam 1990, p. 165; Atil 1990, no. 99 (also in the
    French, Italian and German editions); Swarup 1996, illus. 50;
    al-Qaddūmī 1996, fig. 8b and front cover;
    Bloom and Blair 1997, fig. 220; Khalidi 1999, p. 74

5.2

5.3

5.4

5.3   **BRACELET CLASP**
LNS 208 J
Fabricated from gold, the exterior surfaces worked in *kundan*
   technique and set with rubies, emeralds, diamonds and blue
   sapphires; engraved and chiselled; underside gold sheet,
   engraved
Height 28 mm; length 63 mm;
   width including screw of clasp 24 mm
India, probably Deccan, later 16th–1st third 17th century AD
Gift to the Collection, 1991

5.4   **UPPER ARMBAND (*BĀZŪBAND*)**
LNS 2190 J
Fabricated from gold; worked in *kundan* technique and set
   with rubies, emeralds, diamonds and yellow sapphires;
   engraved and chiselled; interior of plain gold sheet
Height 33 mm; width 67 mm
India, probably Mughal, *c.* 3rd–4th decade 17th century AD
Art market, 1999
Published: Spink, London, October–November 1999, lot 25

5.5   **DAGGER AND SCABBARD**
LNS 300 J
Blade of *jawhar* steel (crudely resharpened); hilt, locket and
   scabbard's sash-cord terminal of nephrite jade (hilt and locket
   pale grey off-white with white flecks, sash-cord terminal
   uniform pale off-white grey), inlaid with gold in *kundan*
   technique and set with rubies and emeralds; the gold quillon
   block worked in *kundan* technique and set with rubies and
   emeralds, engraved and chiselled; scabbard wood overlaid
   with red velvet, and with metal thread trimming
Length of dagger 285 mm; length in scabbard 308 mm;
   width at quillons 57 mm
India, probably Mughal, *c.* 3rd–4th decade 17th century AD
Art market, 1992

5.6

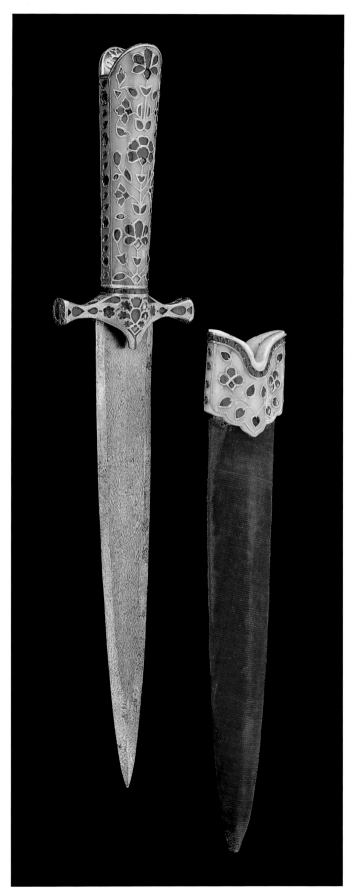

5.5

5.6   PENDANT
LNS 1215 J

Fabricated from gold; the front worked in *kundan*
   technique and set with rubies, emeralds and
   diamonds and engraved and chiselled;
   back, edge and suspension lug champlevé-
   enamelled; with pendant pearl (the latter worn
   almost flat on one side)
Height excluding pendant pearl 38 mm;
   height including pendant pearl 48 mm;
   width 30 mm; thickness 7 mm
India, probably Mughal,
   c. 3rd–5th decade 17th century AD
Art market, 1995

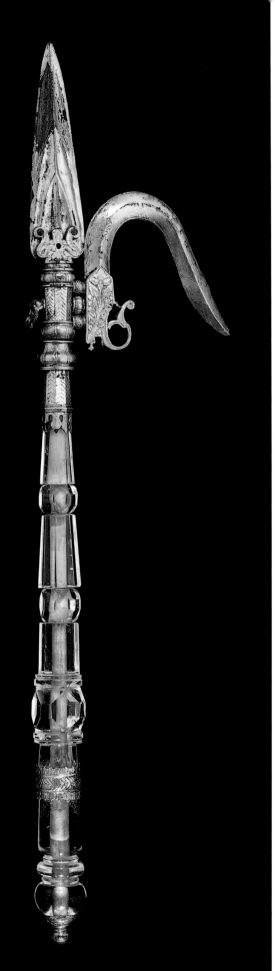

5.7 ELEPHANT GOAD (*ANKUSH*)
LNS 314 M

Blade/hook assemblage, shaft and its finial of forged steel
    with engraved areas, overlaid with partially gilded silver;
    shaft 'threaded' with rock crystal segments, variously
    faceted, carved and drilled
Length 501 mm; width with bail extended 130 mm
India, Mughal or Deccan, *c.* 1st half 17th century AD
Art market, 1992

5.8 LOCKET PENDANT
LNS XV SH

Fabricated from gold, the exterior worked in *kundan* technique,
    set with rubies, emeralds and diamonds and engraved
    (interior plain gold)
Height with bail extended 54 mm;
    width 42 mm; thickness 29 mm
India, Mughal or Deccan, *c.* 1st half 17th century AD
Art market, 1980s

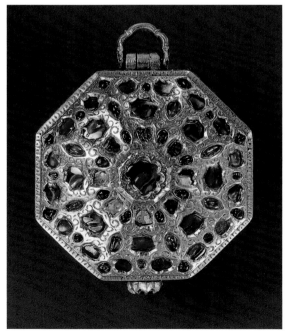

5.9

5.9   **BOX**
LNS 1134 J
Fabricated from gold, the exterior worked in *kundan*
    technique, set with rubies and emeralds and
    engraved (interior plain gold)
Height 31 mm; max. diameter 35 mm
India, Mughal or Deccan, *c.* 1st half 17th century AD
Art market, 1994

5.10   **BOX**
LNS 1802 J
Fabricated from gold, large areas of exterior worked in *kundan* technique and
    set with rubies, diamonds and emeralds; engraved (interior plain gold)
Height 68 mm; diameter 58 mm
India, perhaps Deccan, 18th–19th century AD
Art market, 1997
Published: Spink, London, 1988, no. 68

5.10

6

DEVELOPMENTS IN ENAMELS

Unlike any of the other techniques employed in creating the material presented in this catalogue, enamelling had no relevant background in India or its neighbouring regions whatsoever, being a major jewellers' discipline that was entirely imported, in the persons of European jewellers who came to India in the 16th and earlier 17th centuries. The subsequently demonstrated aptitude, excellence and inventiveness of Indian jewellers in the medium, and its perennial popularity in the Subcontinent, make the facts of its historical background all the more remarkable.

Although some rudimentary enamelling characteristic of the period of classical Graeco-Roman influence in the northwest (for example, at Taxila) is known, this work had no issue, and can be seen to have only the most distant kind of relationship with Mughal-era Indian enamelling. On the other hand, type after type of the enamels of this period can be seen to be based directly on one or more of the highly developed schools of enamelling of Europe, where the continuous lines of evolution over many centuries are quite clear.

The most striking link in the process which resulted in India's artistic efflorescence in the art of enamelling is provided by the al-Sabah Collection's finger ring, Cat. no. 6.1 (LNS 1164 J), in which the form is purely Indian (ultimately derived from Timurid models) while the design and colour scheme are purely European. On the basis of this single example (and a few other not-quite-so-striking but similar instances), evidence of a confluence in the discipline of enamelling between the Indian and European artistic traditions is inescapable. This, of course, should come as no surprise in the light of other arts, such as painting, where such cross-fertilizations are well documented. Similar confluences are particularly to be expected in such fields as the jewelry arts because of the intense interest of the princely classes in these arts and, for example, because of the accounts of the 'artistic delegations' and other contacts between the Mughal court and the Portuguese enclave of Goa during the reign of the emperor Akbar (importantly in the 1570s).

And it would naturally and of necessity be to European masters that Indians would turn for knowledge of enamelling, for not only was the art then at a particularly high level of development in Europe, but, as we have seen, their neighbouring countries had nothing to impart. Most importantly (and contrary to some past assertions in this regard), Iran had no enamelling tradition at all. For this we need not rely only on the negative evidence (no pieces being known), since we also have important specific statements to this effect in the accounts written by both Jean-Baptiste Tavernier and Sir John Chardin. Their evidence is particularly weighty, as each was an experienced traveller in the region and was intimately acquainted with the highest levels of society, as well as being a professional in the jewelry trade.

Despite the lack of a pre-existing tradition of enamelling in India, the art had already become established in the imperial workshops during Akbar's reign: his historian and minister Abu 'l-Fazl speaks of 'cups, flagons, rings and other articles with gold and silver' as being among the products of the enamellers there. Despite this uniquely firm evidence for the establishment of enamelling in Mughal territory, it was probably not the case that it was there that enamelling was first practised in the period, thence to spread to other parts of the Subcontinent. Rather, it is likely that certain centres in the Deccan patronized the art before the Mughals. Be this as it may, from the 16th century onwards, the art of enamelling spread very widely over the Subcontinent, the results of which will provide scholarly endeavour with ample scope for many years to come in the task of isolating and documenting the various regional peculiarities and transregional interrelationships involved.

An outstanding feature of the al-Sabah Collection is its unique ability to convey a sense of the range and distinction of Indian jewellers' achievements in the discipline of enamelling. It is hoped that making this material public will stimulate much serious inquiry into the many questions that its study will raise.

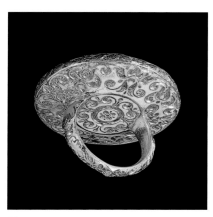

6.1

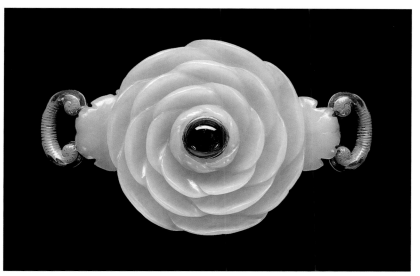

6.2

6.1   FINGER RING
LNS 1164 J
Fabricated from gold; champlevé-enamelled;
    set with a large tourmaline (?) cabochon,
    in replacement of the original stone
Height 28 mm; diameter 34 mm
India, Mughal or Deccan,
    later 16th–earlier 17th century AD
Art market, 1994

6.2   UPPER ARMBAND (*BĀZŪBAND*) CENTREPIECE
LNS 1132 J
Central element carved from nephrite jade (pale greyish green), inlaid with
    gold and set in *kundan* technique with a synthetic ruby cabochon;
    bails gold, champlevé-enamelled
Length including bails 70 mm; diameter of rosette 40 mm; thickness 14 mm
India, Mughal or Deccan, later 16th–earlier 17th century AD
    (ruby and setting modern)
Art market, 1994

6.3   ARCHERY RING
LNS 2216 J
Fabricated from gold; champlevé-enamelled (encrusted),
    set in *kundan* technique with rubies and turquoises
Height 19 mm; length 44 mm; width 31 mm
India, probably Deccan (perhaps Bidar),
    16th–early 17th century AD
Art market, 1999
Published: Christie's, London, 6 October 1999, 2, lot 124

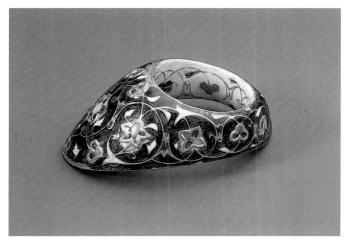

6.3

6.4

6.4 SET OF GAMING PIECES IN THE FORM OF COWRIE SHELLS
LNS 2206 Ja–n
Fabricated from gold, overpainted enamel
  (encrusted, *émail en ronde bosse*)
Average length 19 mm; average width 15 mm
India, Mughal or Deccan,
  later 16th–1st half 17th century AD
Art market, 1999

6.5

6.6

6.5 CUP
LNS 343 J
Fabricated from gold; champlevé- and *basse-taille*-enamelled,
  worked in *kundan* technique and set with rubies and a single
  diamond
Height 19 mm; length 57 mm; width 45 mm
India, probably Mughal, 2nd quarter 17th century AD
Art market, 1992

6.6 ARCHERY RING
LNS 978 J
Cast silver, engraved and champlevé-enamelled, gilded
Height 15 mm; length 42 mm; width 29 mm
India, Deccan, probably Hyderabad, *c.* 1st third 17th century AD
Art market, 1993
Published: Sotheby's, London, 21 October 1993, lot 602

6.7

6.7 ARCHERY RING
LNS 2226 J

Cast silver, engraved and champlevé-enamelled, gilded
Height 15 mm; length 42 mm; width 30 mm
India, Deccan, probably Hyderabad, *c.* 1st third 17th century AD
Art market, 1999
Published: Bonhams, 13 and 14 October 1999, lot 321

6.9

6.9 ARCHERY RING
LNS 1208 J

Cast silver, engraved and champlevé-enamelled, gilded
Height 12 mm; length 44 mm; width 29 mm
India, Deccan, probably Hyderabad, *c.* 1st third 17th century AD
Art market, 1994
Published: Christie's, London, 18 and 20 October 1994, lot 378

6.8

6.8 ARCHERY RING
LNS 1866 J

Cast silver, engraved and champlevé-enamelled, gilded
Height 17 mm; length 43 mm; width 31 mm
India, Deccan, probably Hyderabad, *c.* 1st third 17th century AD
Art market, 1997
Published: Christie's, London, 8 October 1997, lot 396

6.10

6.10 ARCHERY RING
LNS 336 J

Cast silver, engraved, champlevé and *basse-taille* enamels, gilded
Height 16 mm; length 45 mm; width 31 mm
India, Deccan, probably Hyderabad, *c.* 1st third 17th century AD
Art market, 1992

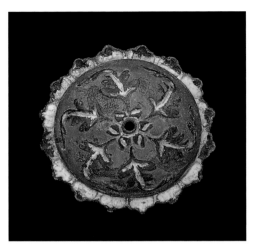

6.11

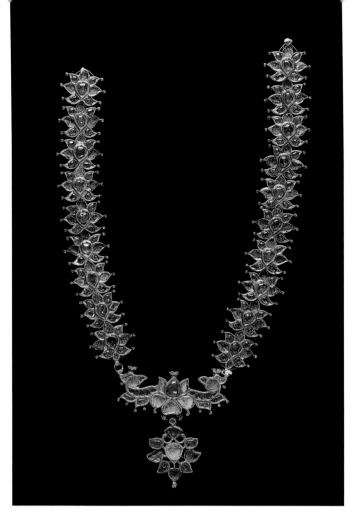

6.11   SHIELD BOSS
LNS 1745 J
Cast copper, champlevé-enamelled, gilded
Height 15 mm; diameter 52 mm
India, Deccan or Mughal, *c.* 3rd–4th decade 17th century AD
Art market, 1997

6.12   NECKLACE
LNS 164 J
Fabricated from gold; champlevé-enamelled (back) and set
     in *kundan* technique with rubies, diamonds and emeralds
Height as illustrated 250 mm;
     average width of 'chain' elements 25 mm;
     width of pendant element 59 mm
India, probably Deccan, *c.* 2nd–3rd decade 17th century AD
Art market, 1980s

6.12

6.14

6.14 RING TO STABILIZE A ROUND-BOTTOMED WATER-PIPE RESERVOIR (*HUQQA*)
LNS 2 J

Hammered up from heavy gold sheet, champlevé-enamelled (small amount of overpainted details), (formerly) set with gemstones in *kundan* technique

Height 33 mm; diameter 146 mm

India, probably Mughal, *c.* 4th decade 17th century AD

Art market, 1981

Published: Jenkins, Keene and Bates 1983, p. 127; Leoshko 1988, fig. 2; Pal et al. 1989, fig. 167; Welch 1985, cat. no. 171; Swarup 1996, illus. 52; Zebrowski 1997, 1, pls 38 and 368

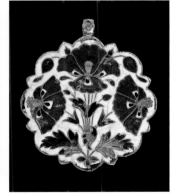

6.15

6.13

6.13 *KATAR* DAGGER
LNS 1743 J

Blade of *jawhar* steel; hilt gold over an iron core, champlevé-enamelled (small amount of overpainted details), set in *kundan* technique with rubies

Length 357 mm; width 87 mm

India, probably Mughal, *c.* 3rd–4th decade 17th century AD

Art market, 1997

6.15 PENDANT
LNS 142 J

Fabricated from gold; worked in *kundan* technique and set with a carved emerald and diamonds; with champlevé enamels

Height 45 mm; width 40 mm; thickness 6 mm

India, probably Mughal, 2nd quarter 17th century AD

Art market, early 1980s

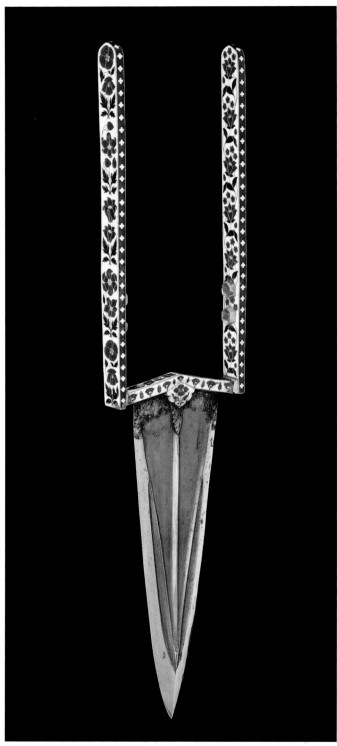

6.16

6.17

6.16   *KATAR* DAGGER
LNS 1822 J
Blade of *jawhar* steel; hilt gold over an iron core,
    champlevé-enamelled (small amount of overpainted details)
Length 420 mm; width 90 mm
India, probably Mughal, 2nd quarter 17th century AD
Art market, 1997

6.17   *KATAR* DAGGER
LNS 1821 J
Blade of *jawhar* steel; hilt gold over an iron core,
    champlevé-enamelled (small amount of overpainted details)
Length 390 mm; width 93 mm
India, probably Mughal, 2nd quarter 17th century AD
Art market, 1997

6.18   *KATAR* DAGGER AND SCABBARD
LNS 222 M

Blade of *jawhar* steel; hilt gold over an iron core, champlevé-
    enamelled; scabbard wood overlaid with green velvet with
    silk and metal thread trimming; chape of gold, champlevé-
    enamelled *en suite* with the hilt

Length of dagger 438 mm; width 91 mm;
    length in scabbard 468 mm; length of chape 32 mm;
    width of chape 14 mm

India, probably Mughal, 2nd quarter 17th century AD

Art market, 1983

Published: Qaddumi 1987, p. 154

6.19   *KATAR* DAGGER AND SCABBARD
LNS 223 M

Blade of *jawhar* steel; hilt gold over an iron core, champlevé-
    enamelled; scabbard wood overlaid with green velvet and metal
    thread trimming; chape of gold, champlevé-enamelled *en suite*
    with the hilt

Length of dagger 400 mm; width 87 mm;
    length in scabbard 413 mm; length of chape 35 mm;
    width of chape 18 mm

India, probably Mughal, *c.* 3rd–5th decade 17th century AD

Art market, 1983

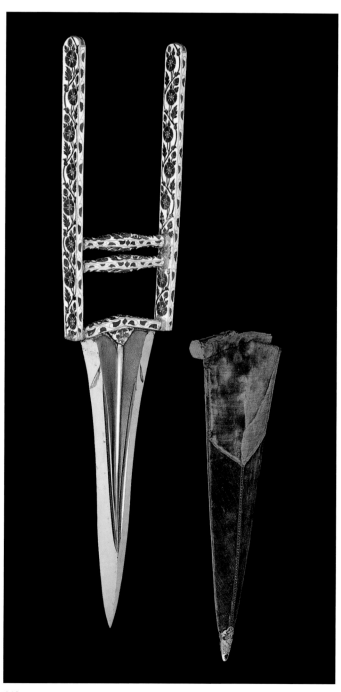

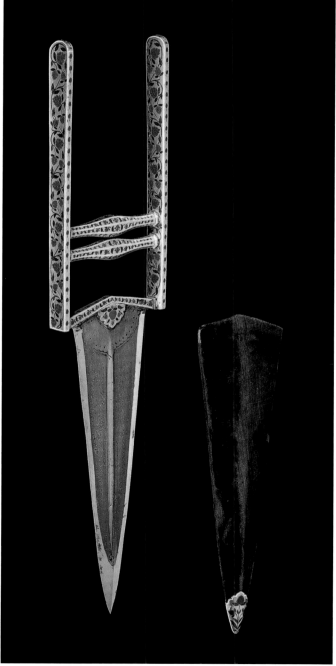

6.18

6.19

6.21

6.21 PENDANT
LNS 1214 J
Fabricated from gold; champlevé-enamelled, set in *kundan*
   technique with rubies and emeralds, and with pendant emerald
Height 45 mm; height including pendant emerald 63 mm;
   width 37 mm; thickness 11 mm
India, probably Mughal, *c*. 4th–5th decade 17th century AD
Art market, 1995

6.20

6.20 BRACELET
LNS 2219 J
Fabricated from gold; champlevé-enamelled, set in *kundan*
   technique with rubies, diamonds and chrysoberyl cat's eye
Diameter 60 mm; diameter of shank 13 mm
India, probably Mughal, *c*. 4th–5th decade 17th century AD
Art market, 1999
Published: Spink, London, 1994, no. 10;
   Christie's, London, 6 October 1999, 2, lot 154

6.22

6.22 NECKLACE TERMINALS
LNS 10 Ja, b
Fabricated from gold; champlevé-enamelled,
   set in *kundan* technique with diamonds
Length 27 mm; width 37 mm
India, Deccan or Mughal, *c*. 1st half 17th century AD
Art market, 1979

6.23

6.24

6.25

6.23 NECKLACE
LNS 102 J
    Fabricated from gold; worked in *kundan* technique and
        set with rubies and emeralds; with champlevé enamels;
        strung with pearls
    Overall height 280 mm; width 228 mm;
        average max. dimensions of terminals 24 × 20 × 5 mm
    India, probably Mughal, *c*. 5th–6th decade 17th century AD
    Art market, 1979

6.24 PENDANT
LNS 1213 J
    Fabricated from gold; champlevé-enamelled, set in *kundan*
        technique with rubies, emeralds and diamonds
    Height 42 mm; width 32 mm; thickness 10 mm
    India, Deccan or Mughal, *c*. 4th–5th decade 17th century AD
    Art market, 1995

6.25 PENDANT
LNS 2199 J
    Fabricated from gold; champlevé-enamelled, set in *kundan*
        technique with rubies, emeralds and diamonds;
        with pendant emerald
    Height 42 mm; height including pendant emerald 59 mm;
        width 35 mm; thickness 9 mm
    India, Deccan or Mughal, *c*. 4th–5th decade 17th century AD
    Art market, 1999

6.26

6.26 SWORD, SCABBARD, LOCKET AND CHAPE
LNS 1016 Ma, b

Blade of *jawhar* steel; hilt gold over an iron core, champlevé-
    enamelled; scabbard wood overlaid with carmine velvet
    with metal thread trimming
Length of sword 880 mm; width at quillons 84 mm;
    length in scabbard 940 mm; length of locket 77 mm;
    length of chape 71 mm
India, Deccan or Mughal, *c.* mid-17th century AD
Art market, 1999
Published: Christie's, London, 19 and 20 April 1999, lot 407

6.27 BOX
LNS 1651 J

Fabricated from gold, champlevé-enamelled, set in *kundan*
    technique with rubies, emeralds and diamonds
Height 27 mm; diameter 47 mm;
    width including hinge and hasp 57 mm
India, Deccan or Mughal, *c.* 4th–5th decade 17th century AD
Art market, 1997

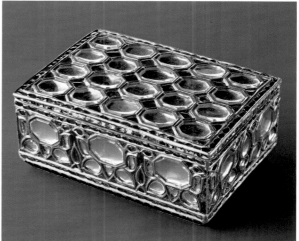

6.28

6.28 BOX
LNS 2004 J

Fabricated from gold, champlevé-enamelled, set in *kundan*
    technique with rubies and rock crystals
Height 26 mm; length 62 mm; width 49 mm
India, Deccan or Mughal, *c.* 4th–5th decade 17th century AD
Art market, 1998

6.27

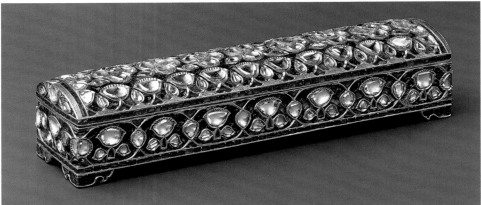

6.29

6.29 BOX
LNS 1135 J
Fabricated from gold,
champlevé- and *basse-taille-*
enamelled, set in *kundan*
technique with rubies,
emeralds and diamonds
Height including lid 29 mm;
length 131 mm; width 31 mm
India, Deccan or Mughal,
c. 4th–5th decade
17th century AD
Art market, 1994

6.30 PENDANT
LNS 956 J
Fabricated from gold; champlevé-enamelled,
set in *kundan* technique with rubies
and diamonds; with pendant pearl
Height 30 mm;
height including pendant pearl 44 mm;
thickness 6 mm
India, Deccan or Mughal,
probably 2nd quarter 17th century AD
Art market, 1993

6.30

6.31 SIX HARNESS FITTINGS
LNS 260 Ja–f
Fabricated from gold; champlevé-enamelled,
set in *kundan* technique with diamonds
and emeralds
Average measurements of domical fittings,
height 28 mm, diameter 57 mm;
buckle 57 × 37 × 6 mm;
average measurements of strap holders,
47 × 14 × 11 mm
India, Mughal or Deccan,
c. 3rd quarter 17th century AD
Art market, 1991

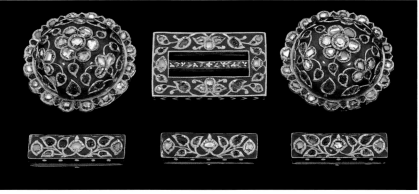

6.31

6.32 SWORD, SCABBARD, LOCKET AND CHAPE LNS 2157 Ja, b

Blade steel (probably *jawhar*, but obscured by repolishing); hilt gold over an iron core, champlevé-enamelled, set in *kundan* technique with diamonds and emeralds; scabbard wood overlaid with velvet; locket and chape champlevé-enamelled, set in *kundan* technique with diamonds and emeralds

Length of sword with bail folded 860 mm; width at quillons 101 mm; diameter of disc 72 mm; length in scabbard with bail folded 890 mm; length of locket 84 mm; width of locket 50 mm; length of chape 96 mm; width of chape 42 mm

India, Mughal or Deccan, *c.* 3rd–4th quarter 17th century AD

Art market, 1999

Published: Habsburg, Feldman, Geneva, 29 June 1988, lot 51/285

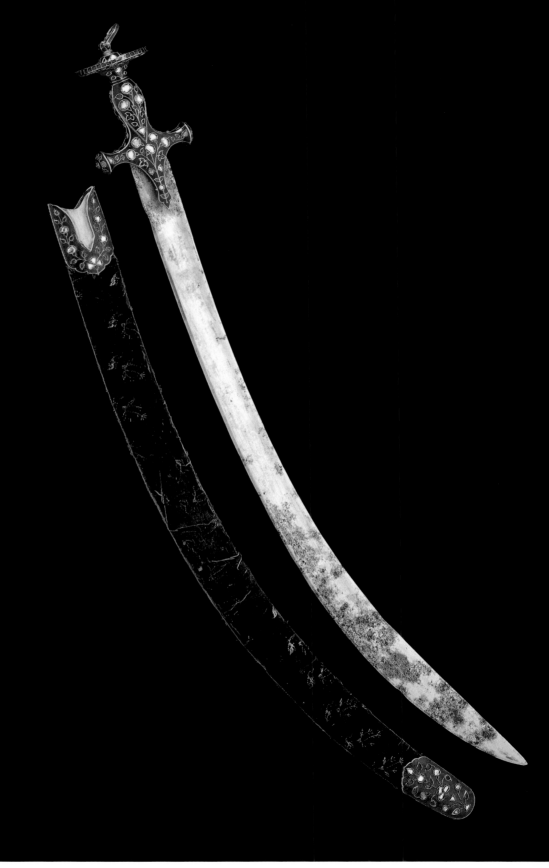

6.32

6.33a, b

6.33a MINIATURE MANUSCRIPT OF THE QUR'AN
LNS 373 HS

Manuscript inscribed in black ink on paper,
   illumination in ink, gold and colours; binding
   slabs of nephrite jade (white, with slight
   greyish cast), inlaid with gold and set in
   kundan technique with rubies and emeralds;
   the leather spine painted in gold
Height 94 mm; width 57 mm; thickness 19 mm
India, Deccan or Mughal,
   dated AH 1085/AD 1674–75
Art market, 1999
Published: Sotheby's, London, 24 April 1996,
   lot 10

6.33b PENDANT CASE FOR A QUR'AN MANUSCRIPT (probably made for and contemporaneous with 6.33a, dated AH 1085/AD 1674–75)
LNS 2201 J

Fabricated from gold; champlevé-enamelled,
   set in *kundan* technique with diamonds,
   rubies and emeralds
Height 79 mm; width 100 mm; thickness 23 mm
India, Deccan or Mughal,
   probably eighth decade 17th century AD
Art market, 1999

6.34 PENDANT
LNS 958 J

Fabricated from gold; champlevé-enamelled,
   set in *kundan* technique with diamonds,
   emeralds and a single ruby; with pendant
   emerald
Height 48 mm; height including pendant
   emerald 64 mm; thickness 10 mm
India, Deccan or Mughal,
   c. 3rd–4th quarter 17th century AD
Art market, 1993

6.34

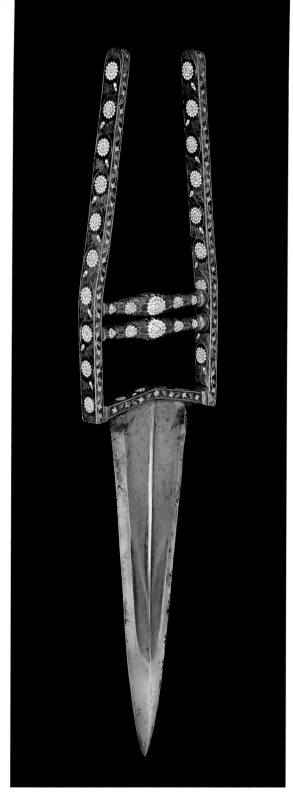

6.35

6.36   DAGGER AND SCABBARD
LNS 1004 M

Blade of *jawhar* steel; hilt silver over an iron core, with champlevé and
    painted enamels; scabbard wood covered with leather, lacquer-painted;
    locket and chape silver, with champlevé and painted enamels
Length 406 mm; length in scabbard 430 mm; width 92 mm; thickness 42 mm
India, Deccan or Mughal, probably *c.* 3rd–4th quarter 17th century AD
Art market, 1998
Ex coll.: The Harry W. Bass Jr. Research Foundation, Texas
Published: Christie's, London, 13 October 1998, lot 113

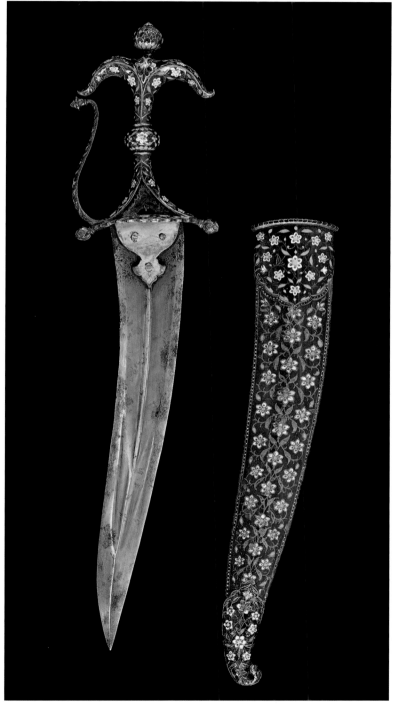

6.36

6.35   *KATAR* DAGGER
LNS 169 M

Blade of *jawhar* steel; hilt silver over an iron core,
    with champlevé and painted enamels, gilded
Length 418 mm; width 88 mm
India, Deccan or Mughal,
    c. 2nd–3rd quarter 17th century AD
Art market, 1982

6.37

6.38

6.37 LOCKET AND CHAPE
LNS 2160 Ja, b
Fabricated from gold,
    champlevé-enamelled
Length of locket 80 mm;
    width including lug 60 mm;
    length of chape 130 mm;
    width 40 mm
India, Deccan or Mughal,
    probably *c*. 3rd quarter
    17th century AD
Art market, 1999

6.38 LIDDED CUP AND SAUCER
LNS 2191 Ja–c
Fabricated from gold, with champlevé and painted enamels
Height of assembled pieces 82 mm; height of lidded cup 78 mm;
    diameter of lidded cup 72 mm; height of saucer 13 mm;
    diameter of saucer 129 mm
India, Deccan or Mughal, probably *c*. mid-17th century AD
Art market, 1999
Ex coll.: The Marquesses of Bute
Published: Christie's, London, 3 July 1996, lot 26; Zebrowski 1997, 1, pl. 60;
    Zebrowski 1997, 2, fig. 19; Spink, London, October–November 1999, no. 26

6.39 SWORD, SCABBARD AND CHAPE
LNS 2193 Ja, b
Blade of *jawhar* steel, inlaid with gold; hilt gold over an iron core, champlevé-enamelled
    and set in *kundan* technique with diamonds, rubies and emeralds; scabbard wood overlaid
    with purple velvet with metal thread trimming; chape gold, champlevé-enamelled and set
    in *kundan* technique with diamonds, rubies and emeralds
Length of sword 880 mm; length in scabbard 900 mm; width at quillons 101 mm;
    diameter of disc 71 mm; length of chape 97 mm; width of chape 33 mm
India, Deccan or Mughal, *c*. 3rd–4th quarter 17th century AD
Art market, 1999
Published: Christie's, London, 13 October 1998, lot 134

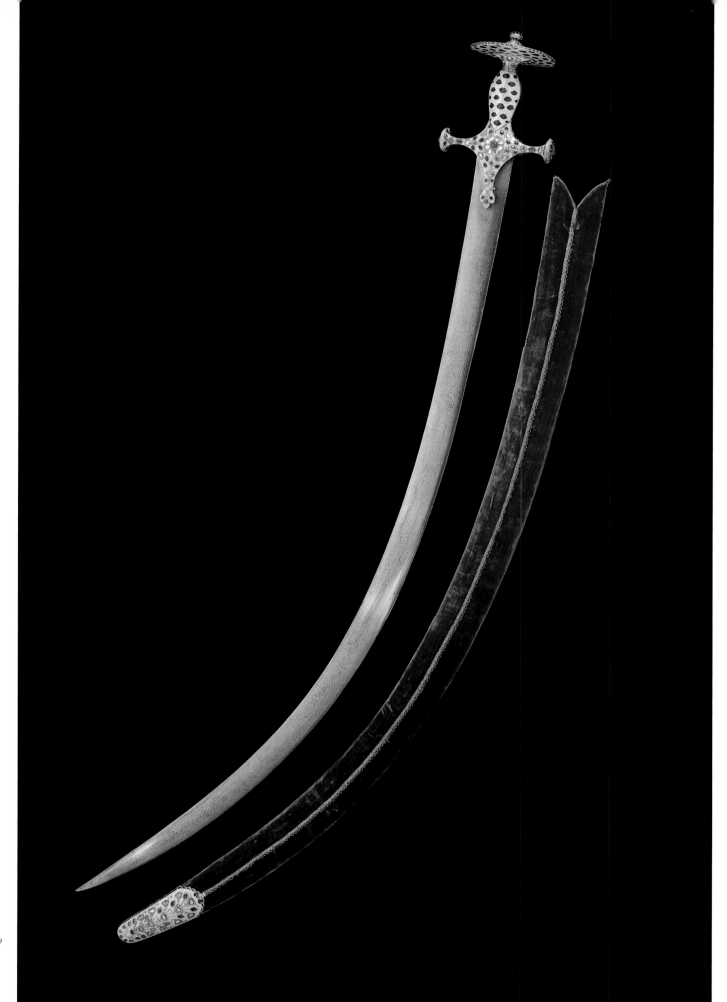

6.40

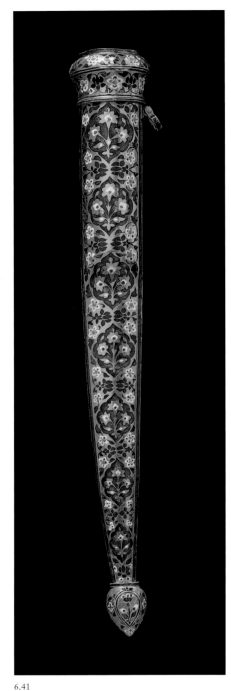

6.41

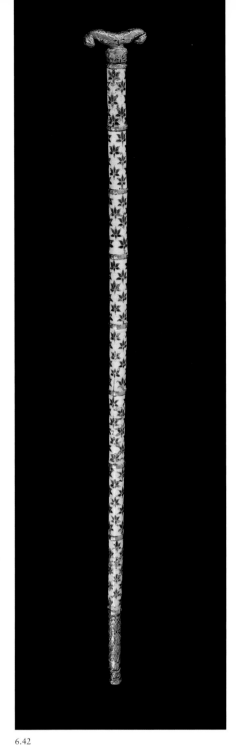

6.42

6.40   SCABBARD
LNS 1658 J
Fabricated from gold, with
    champlevé and painted enamels
Length 311 mm;
    width with bail folded 43 mm
India, Sind, perhaps earlier
    18th century AD
Art market, 1996
Published: Sotheby's, New York,
    19 September 1996, lot 222

6.41   SCABBARD
LNS 27 J
Fabricated from gold,
    champlevé-enamelled
Length 316 mm;
    width with bail folded 44 mm
India, Sind, probably 18th century AD
Art market 1980s

**6.42   MINIATURE CRUTCH
('ZAFAR TAKĪYA')**
LNS 286 M
Gold, champlevé-enamelled
Length 370 mm; width 33 mm
India, Mughal or Deccan, 2nd half
    17th–early 18th century AD
Art market, 1989

6.43

6.43   PAIR OF BRACELETS
LNS 1863 Ja, b

Fabricated from gold, with champlevé and painted enamels, set in *kundan* technique
   with diamonds, rubies and emeralds

Average height 57 mm; average width 58 mm;
   average thickness including clasp screw 12 mm

India, probably Mughal, 2nd half 17th–early 18th century AD

Art market, 1997

Published: Christie's, London, 8 October 1997, lot 319

6.45

6.45   BRACELET
LNS 1812 J

Fabricated from gold, champlevé-
   enamelled; set in *kundan* technique
   with diamonds, rubies and glass

Height 89 mm; width 88 mm;
   thickness 20 mm

India, probably Deccan,
   late 17th–18th century AD

Art market, 1997

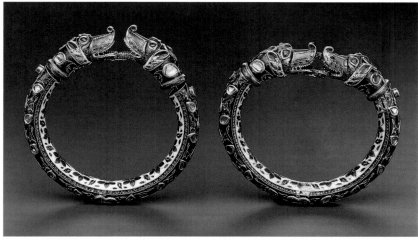

6.44

6.44   PAIR OF BRACELETS
LNS 1864 Ja, b

Fabricated from gold, champlevé-enamelled; set in *kundan* technique with diamonds
   and rubies

Average height 88 mm; average width 86 mm; thickness including clasp screw 18 mm

India, probably Mughal, later 17th–early 18th century AD

Art market, 1997

Published: Christie's, London, 8 October 1997, lot 323

6.46

6.48

6.46   PAIR OF TOE RINGS
LNS 210 Ja, b
Fabricated from gold and silver, champlevé-enamelled,
    set in *kundan* technique with rubies
Average diameter 33 mm; average width 13 mm
India, probably Deccan, late 17th–18th century AD
Art market, 1991

6.48   BOX
LNS 2175 J
Fabricated from gold, champlevé- and *basse-taille*-enamelled,
    set in *kundan* technique with diamonds and rubies
Height 33 mm; length 67 mm; width 49 mm
India, probably Deccan, 18th century AD
Art market, 1999

6.47

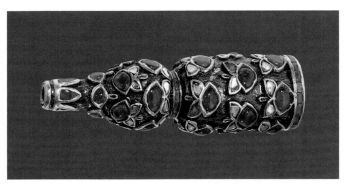

6.49

6.47   ARCHERY RING
LNS 1136 J
Fabricated from gold, with champlevé and painted enamels;
    set in *kundan* technique with a spinel
Height 19 mm; length 49 mm; width 29 mm
India, probably Hyderabad (Deccan), *c.* 1700 AD
Art market, 1994

6.49   MOUTHPIECE FOR A WATER-PIPE
(*HUQQA*) HOSE
LNS 171 J
Fabricated from gold, champlevé-enamelled, set in *kundan*
    technique with diamonds and rubies
Length 67 mm; diameter 22 mm
India, probably Hyderabad (Deccan), late 17th–18th century AD
Art market, 1990

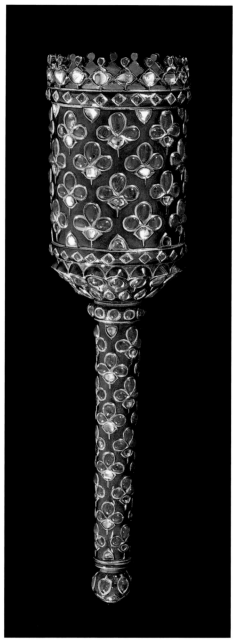

6.50

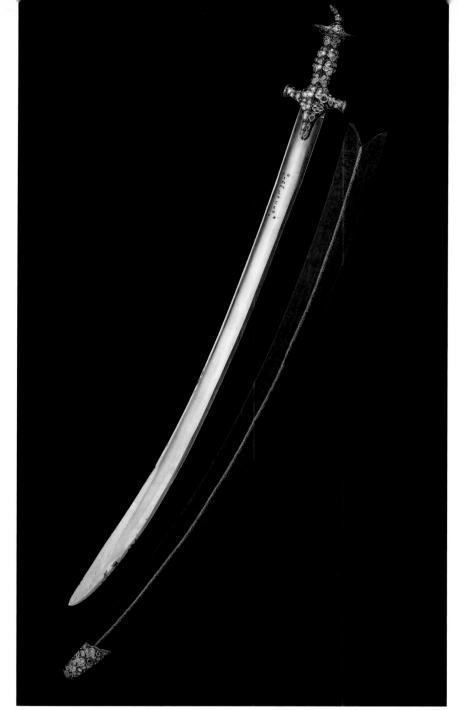

6.51

6.50 **FLYWHISK HANDLE**
LNS 1805 J
Fabricated from gold, champlevé-
    enamelled, set in *kundan* technique
    with diamonds and rubies
Length 255 mm; diameter 65 mm
India, probably Hyderabad (Deccan),
    18th century AD
Art market, 1997

6.51 **SWORD, SCABBARD AND CHAPE**
LNS 2154 Ja, b
Blade steel (repolished), stamped with 'European' type marks, the spine with a punch-
    marked *Devanagari* inscription; hilt gold over an iron core, champlevé-enamelled,
    set in *kundan* technique with diamonds and rubies; scabbard wood overlaid with
    purple velvet with metal thread trimming; chape gold, champlevé-enamelled,
    set in *kundan* technique with diamonds
Length of sword with bail folded 885 mm; length in scabbard with bail folded 975 mm;
    width at quillons 86 mm; diameter of disc 60 mm; length of chape 75 mm;
    width of chape 38 mm
India, Hyderabad (Deccan), end 18th century AD
    (dated in the enamelwork AH 1213/AD 1798–99)
Art market, 1998
Published: Bonhams, 14 October 1998, lot 231

6.52 DAGGER, SCABBARD, LOCKET AND CHAPE
LNS 26 Ja, b

Blade steel, repolished; hilt gold over an
    iron core, champlevé-enamelled, set in
    kundan technique with diamonds and
    rubies; scabbard wood overlaid with red
    velvet with metal thread trimming
Length of dagger 370 mm;
    length in scabbard 385 mm;
    width 81 mm
India, probably Hyderabad (Deccan),
    18th century AD
Art market, 1980s
Published: Jenkins, Keene and Bates 1983,
    p. 128

6.53

6.55

6.53   PAIR OF BRACELETS
LNS 18 Ja, b

Fabricated from gold, champlevé-enamelled, set in *kundan*
    technique with diamonds
Average diameter 79 mm; average thickness of shank 14 mm;
    average width of shank 15 mm
India, probably Hyderabad (Deccan), 18th–early 19th century AD
Art market, 1979

6.55   BRACELET
LNS 162 J

Fabricated from gold, champlevé-enamelled, set in *kundan*
    technique with diamonds, rubies and a spinel
Length of centrepiece 56 mm; width 41 mm;
    length of 'shank' removed from clasp 135 mm; width 23 mm
India, Deccan, Bijapur or Hyderabad, probably 18th century AD
Art market, 1979

6.54

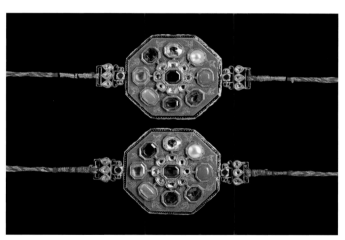

6.56

6.54   BOX
LNS 1806 J

Fabricated from gold, with champlevé and overpainted enamels
Height 20 mm; length 46 mm; width 40 mm
India, probably Hyderabad (Deccan), 18th–early 19th century AD
Art market, 1999

6.56   PAIR OF UPPER ARMBANDS (*BĀZŪBANDS*)
SET WITH THE NINE AUSPICIOUS GEMS OR
NAVARATNA
LNS 340 Ja, b

Fabricated from gold, champlevé-enamelled, set in *kundan*
    technique with ruby, diamonds, pearl, coral, zircon, blue
    sapphire, chrysoberyl cat's eye, yellow topaz and emerald;
    each fitted with a pair of cords of silk and metallic threads,
    for binding to the arm
Average length (not including cord) 66 mm; average width 37 mm;
    average thickness 8 mm
India (perhaps Hyderabad, Deccan), 18th–early 19th century AD
Art market, 1992

7

GOLD-EMBELLISHED STEEL

So-called 'oriental' arms and armour are legendary for damascening, a term used to refer to both the inlay and the overlay of steel with precious-metal decoration (usually gold). In such embellishment, as with other aspects of arts and crafts in general and with other disciplines connected with iron and steel in particular, India excelled.

The inlaying and overlaying of iron and steel articles has a long history in Asia and Egypt, as well as in Europe. The Mughal-period manifestations of such decoration continue a tradition which had its beginnings in Iran during the medieval period. As we have suggested in the case of the inlaying of hardstones (see page 30), this was probably inspired by, or at least received fresh impetus from, the rise and florescence in eastern Iran (especially Herat) in the 12th and early 13th centuries of a very sophisticated, significant and celebrated school of the inlaying of copper-alloy vessels with silver and copper. Evidence that such inlay of weapons reached a high level of excellence in this period is supplied by a series of knives and daggers in the al-Sabah Collection (not illustrated here due to space constraints).

The very finest work of the Mughal era, like the medieval examples just mentioned, is executed in inlay, in which grooves forming the lines of the design are cut in such a way as to leave gripping configurations in the cavities, into which the precious metal is then hammered and becomes locked into place. It appears that this technique was practised with special finesse and was particularly prevalent in the Deccan.

Although we have drawn attention to the special quality of inlaid decoration, we must also point out that some of the most beautiful pieces of the period (for example, the daggers, Cat. no. 1.12 [LNS 2221 J] and Cat. no. 5.2 [LNS 25 J]) have their blades decorated not in inlay but in overlay. In this technique, the overall surface to be decorated is first hatched with a sharp-bladed chisel and the design, in the form of precious-metal wire, is then hammered, with remarkable precision, on to the hatching.

In general, such decoration, in which the precious metal (almost invariably gold) stands out in contrast against the dark iron or steel surface (which is blued or otherwise patinated), is very effective. It is especially so when designed and executed by such gifted masters as those who practised the craft during the period with which we are concerned.

In Mughal India during the reign of the emperor Akbar (and, no doubt, also later and in non-Mughal territory), the inlayers of steel were ranked equal to the inlayers of hardstones, being designated by the same term (*zar-nishān*) and receiving the same level of pay – among the highest mentioned for precious-material craftsmen by Akbar's minister and historian, Abu 'l-Fazl. These artists are well represented by the superb examples presented here.

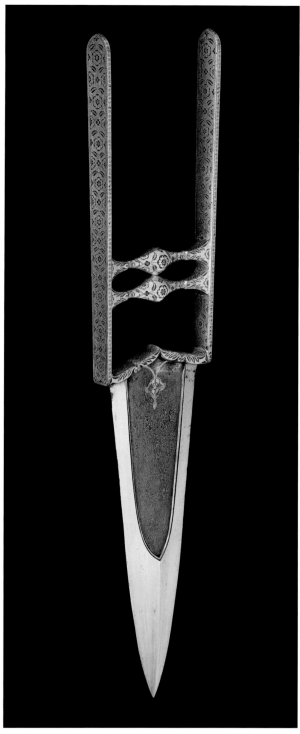

7.1

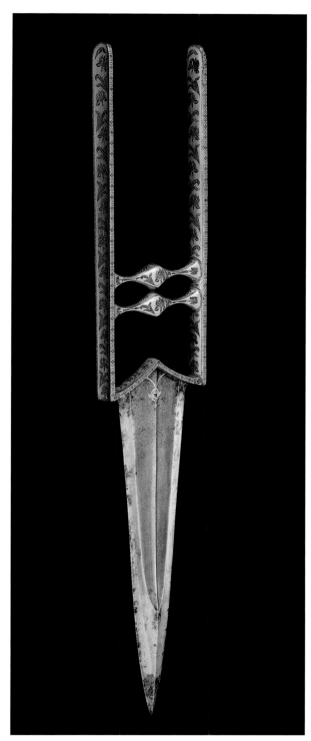

7.2

7.1 *KATAR* DAGGER
LNS 303 M
Blade of *jawhar* steel, inlaid with gold;
 hilt of patinated steel inlaid with gold
Length 442 mm; width 90 mm
India, Deccan or Mughal,
 probably *c.* 2nd quarter 17th century AD
Art market, 1991

7.2 *KATAR* DAGGER
LNS 901 M
Blade of *jawhar* steel, inlaid with gold;
 hilt of patinated steel inlaid with gold
Length 440 mm; width 80 mm
India, Deccan or Mughal, *c.* mid-17th century AD
Art market, 1997
Published: Christie's, London, 14 October 1997, lot 222

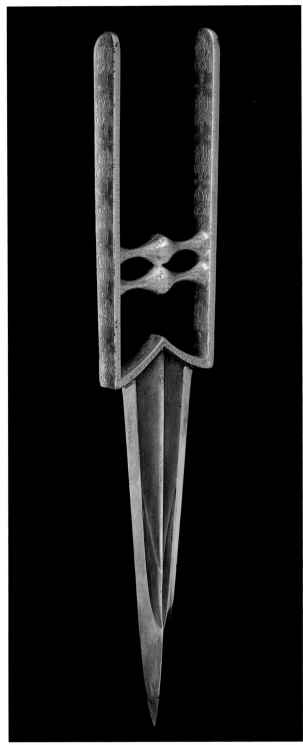

7.3

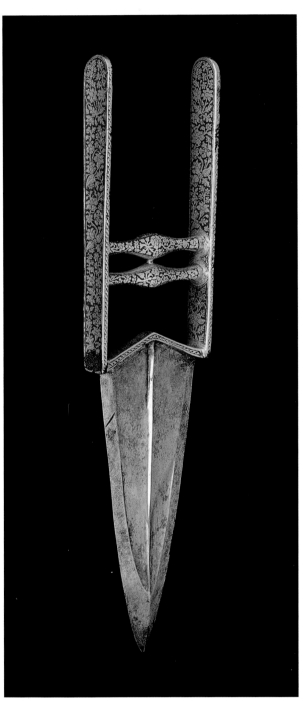

7.4

7.3   *KATAR* DAGGER
LNS 304 M

Blade of *jawhar* steel; hilt steel, overlaid with gold in two colours,
   the latter tooled, including ringmatting of the ground
Length 448 mm; width 83 mm
India, Deccan or Mughal, *c.* mid-17th century AD
Art market, 1991

7.4   *KATAR* DAGGER
LNS 902 M

Blade steel, repolished; hilt steel overlaid with gold
Length 346 mm; width 80 mm
India, Deccan (perhaps Bijapur), *c.* 1st half 17th century AD
Art market, 1997
Published: Christie's, London, 14 October 1997, lot 231

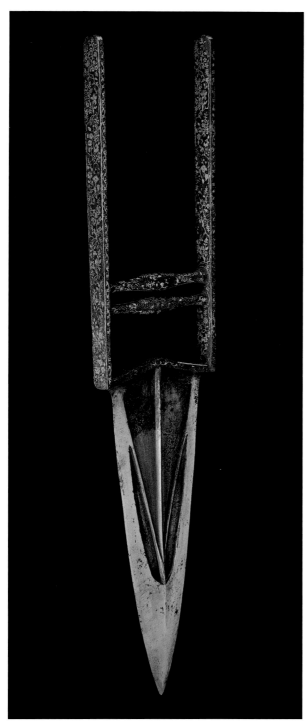

7.5

7.6

7.6   HORSE STRAP FITTING
LNS 151 J
Steel, overlaid with two colours of gold
Diameter 44 mm; thickness 10 mm
India, probably Deccan,
        c. 2nd–3rd quarter 17th century AD
Art market, 1988

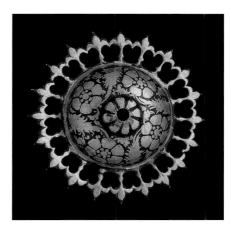

7.7

7.5   *KATAR* DAGGER
LNS 1008 M
Blade of *jawhar* steel; hilt steel, inlaid with two colours
        of gold and silver
Length 421 mm; width 88 mm
India, probably Deccan, *c*. 2nd quarter 17th century AD
Art market, 1998
Published: Christie's, London, 28 April 1998, lot 134;
        Bonhams, 14 October 1998, lot 223

7.7   SHIELD BOSS
LNS 312 M
Steel, overlaid with gold
Diameter 51 mm; thickness 12 mm
India, Deccan (perhaps Hyderabad),
        17th century AD
Art market, 1991

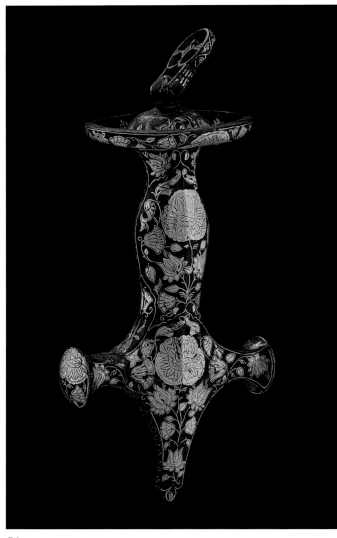

7.8

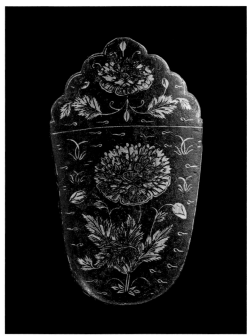

7.9

7.8 **SWORD HILT**
LNS 295 M
Steel, inlaid with gold
Length of hilt with the bail folded 160 mm;
    width at quillons 81 mm; diameter of disc 59 mm
India, Deccan (probably Hyderabad), 17th century AD
Art market, 1991

7.9 **CHAPE**
LNS 311 M
Steel, inlaid with gold
Length 64 mm; width 35 mm
India, Deccan (probably Hyderabad),
    c. 2nd–3rd quarter 17th century AD
Art market, 1991

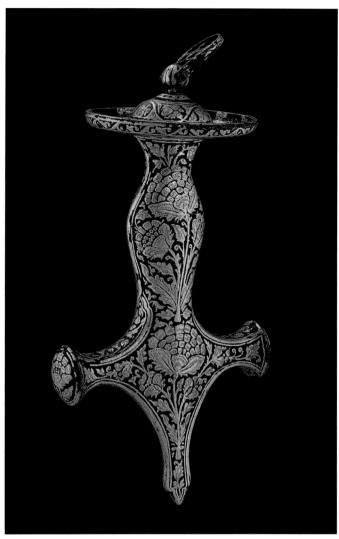

7.10

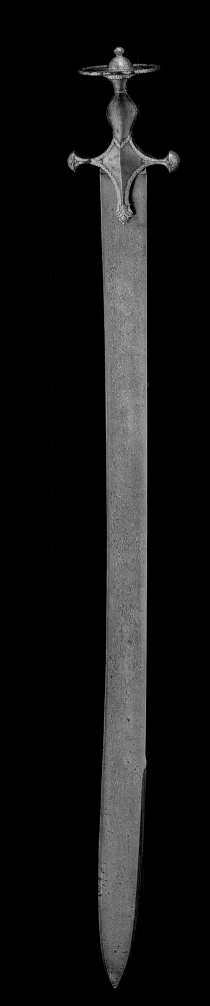

7.10 SWORD HILT
LNS 297 M

Steel, overlaid with gold

Length of hilt with the bail folded 162 mm;
    width at quillons 81 mm; diameter of disc 59 mm

India, Deccan (perhaps Hyderabad),
    c. 2nd–3rd quarter 17th century AD

Art market, 1991

7.11 SWORD
LNS 282 M

Blade and hilt of *jawhar* steel, the latter overlaid with gold

Length 1,038 mm; width at quillons 109 mm; diameter of disc 77 mm

India, probably North, later 17th–early 18th century AD

Art market, 1980s

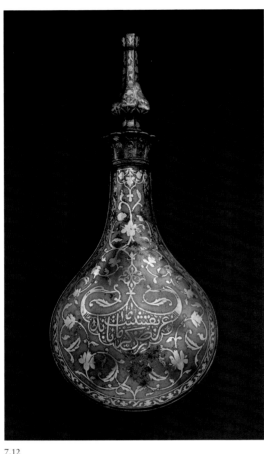

7.12

7.12 GUNPOWDER FLASK
LNS 141 M
Steel, overlaid with gold
Length 188 mm; width 79 mm
India, Deccan (probably Hyderabad), *c.* 2nd quarter 17th century AD
Art market, 1981
Published: Qaddumi 1987, p. 152; Atil 1990, no. 94 (also in the French,
    Italian, German, Portuguese and Arabic editions)

7.13 GUN-BARREL REST
LNS 186 M
Steel, inlaid with gold, with silver rosette 'washers'
Length with barrel rest in upright position 396 mm; width 108 mm
India, Mughal or Deccan, 17th century AD
Art market, 1980s

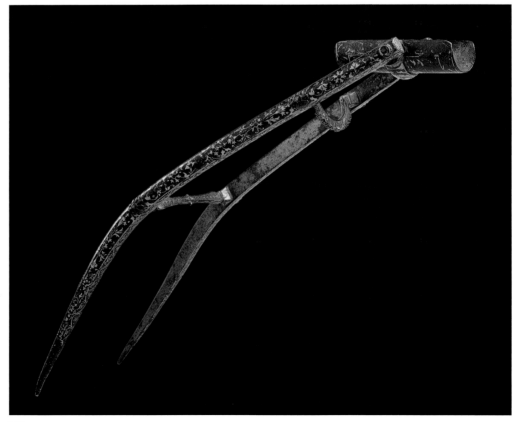

7.13

7.14   *KATAR* DAGGER
LNS 185 M

Blade steel, repolished, and with etched *Devanagari* inscription;
  hilt steel, overlaid with copper, the latter inlaid with silver
  and gold
Length 457 mm; width 88 mm
India, Deccan or Mughal, 2nd half 17th–early 18th century AD
Art market, 1980s

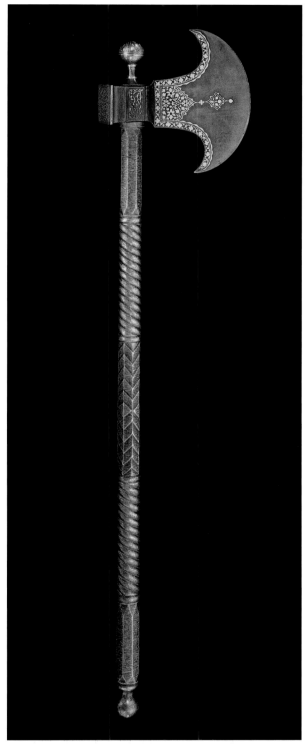

7.15

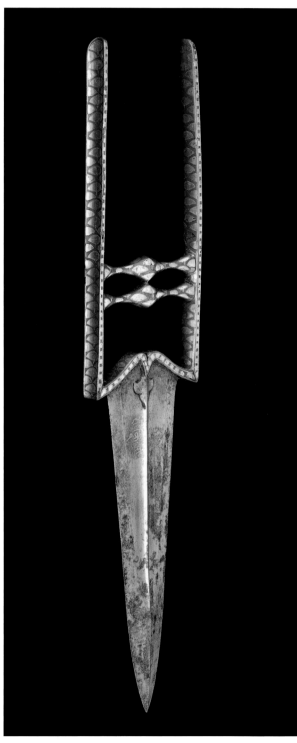

7.14

7.15   SADDLE-AXE
LNS 729 M

Fabricated entirely from *jawhar* steel, overlaid with gold
Length 723 mm; width 155 mm
India, probably Deccan, 2nd half 17th–early 18th century AD
Art market, 1995
Published: Sotheby's, London, 27 April 1995, lot 102

8

THREE-DIMENSIONAL EXPRESSIONS

To the extent that the arts of India during the Mughal period form a branch of 'Islamic art', it is a branch unique in many ways, one of the most important of which is the manifestation of the national penchant for plastic expression. This is perhaps most clearly seen in the character of Indian miniature paintings, particularly those produced under the Mughals and some of their successor schools.

It cannot, however, be too strongly emphasized that there is no truth whatever in the suggestion that Islamic art, in any period or region, is characterized by the absence of sculpture in the true sense of the word. Leaving aside the vast number of statues and figurines (which latter, especially, proliferated over vast stretches of the Islamic world), this civilization has produced a huge corpus of sculptural objects of notable distinction, an output difficult to parallel in any other time or region. Most typically, this tradition is represented by objects of utility, such as vessels of various materials, but the same outstanding formal sense was expressed in all aspects of life, from architecture to costume and to all manner of personal belongings and adornment.

It was the fear of idolatry that initially raised religious objections to statuary – a concern not unique to Islam, particularly at the time. However, even at its most resolute, such concerns did not inhibit non-representational sculptural expression. And since the sculptural impulse is arguably the most fundamental of all plastic-arts impulses, it gave rise to an enormous and rich body of abstract sculptural forms in Islam.

The combination of Islamic art's far-reaching and uniquely developed traditions of sophisticated design on the one hand, and India's special feeling for form on the other, produced a continuing series of particularly satisfying objects. In early Islamic times, India contributed to the formation of Islamic art's developing traditions of design, and long before the Mughal period large swaths of India shared in the development of those traditions.

Another of India's perennial tastes, the delight in the multiplication of elements in artistic compositions – dizzying perhaps to the uninitiated but, like the years and gods in their traditional cosmologies and pantheons, totally organized – has often been a stumbling block to the proper appreciation of Indian jewelled arts. This is often true of Islamic-art specialists, as well as of the general public, particularly in the West. That the sculptural expression in Indian objects of the Mughal period could be as pure and simple as the simplest of modern abstract sculpture will be seen in some of the examples in this group of pieces; and we can only encourage anyone inclined to negative reactions when confronted with the more elaborate productions to take the time to absorb them fully, with the promise that they will be found to be under complete artistic control, evocative of a sophisticated sensibility and, furthermore, testimony to astounding technique.

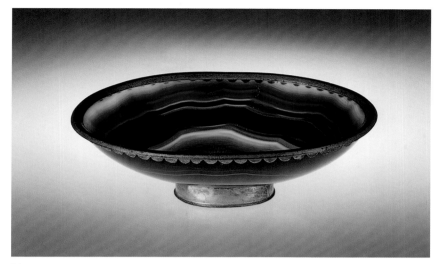

8.1

8.1   BOWL
LNS 65 HS
Carved from banded agate; with gilded bronze fittings
Height 40 mm; length 123 mm; width 88 mm
India, probably Cambay, *c.* 16th century AD
Art market, 1991
Published: Sotheby's, London, 24 and 25 April 1991, lot 671

8.2   BOWL
LNS 63 HS
Carved from nephrite jade (predominantly
    variegated olive green, with black flecks
    and white and pink mottling)
Height 44 mm; length 87 mm; width 72 mm
India, perhaps Deccan, 17th century or earlier
Art market, 1990

8.2

8.3   BOWL
LNS 48 HS
Carved from rock crystal; with repoussé-
    worked gilded silver mounts
Height 91 mm; length 240 mm; width 165 mm
Bowl India, Mughal or Deccan,
    c. mid-17th century AD;
    mounts Tibetan, 18th century AD
Art market, 1980s
Published: Atil 1994, p. 322 (also in the
    German, Portuguese and Arabic editions)

8.3

8.4

8.6

8.4 BOWL
LNS 355 HS
Carved from nephrite jade (greyish green with some subtle whitish mottling)
Height 63 mm; length 202 mm; width 122 mm
India, Mughal or Deccan, *c.* mid-17th century AD
Art market, 1998
Published: Sotheby's, London, 15 October 1998, 1, lot 115

8.6 CUP
LNS 325 HS
Carved from nephrite jade (translucent white
 with cloudlike variegations)
Height 21 mm; length including handle 77 mm;
 diameter 65 mm
India, Deccan or Mughal,
 c. mid-17th century AD
Art market, 1998

8.5

8.7

8.5 BOWL
LNS 375 HS
Carved from nephrite jade (greyish green, with black flecks and russet areas)
Height 46 mm; length 186 mm; width 118 mm
India, Mughal or Deccan, *c.* mid-17th century AD
Art market, 1999
Published: Sotheby's, London, 14 October 1999, 1, lot 163

8.7 CUP
LNS 326 HS
Carved from nephrite jade (translucent off-white
 with russet areas)
Height 15 mm; length including handle 75 mm;
 diameter 65 mm
India, Deccan or Mughal,
 c. mid-17th century AD
Art market, 1998

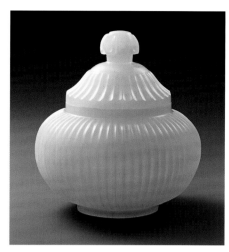

8.8

8.8　LIDDED POT
LNS 240 HS

Carved from nephrite jade (white, of
　　great uniformity and translucency)
Height 77 mm; diameter 69 mm
India, probably Deccan, 17th century AD
Art market, 1996
Published: Christie's, South Kensington,
　　27 June 1996, lot 261

8.9　CEREMONIAL STAFF
　　　　(BACK-SCRATCHER)
LNS 319 HS

Carved from nephrite jade (irregularly
　　variegated, from a near-black green
　　to light yellowish green, with flecks
　　and veins); the shaft segments
　　threaded on an iron rod; with silver
　　and gilded bronze fittings
Length 612 mm; width 48 mm
India, probably Deccan, 17th century AD
Art market, 1998

8.9

8.10

8.10　BOX
LNS 218 HS

Carved from nephrite jade (irregularly variegated, from a near
　　black green to light yellowish green, with flecks and veins);
　　gold hinge; traces of floral decoration on lid
Height 42 mm; length 148 mm; width 101 mm
India, probably Deccan, 17th century AD
Art market, 1994

8.11

8.11　DISH
LNS 219 HS

Carved from nephrite jade (irregularly variegated, from a
　　near-black green to light yellowish green, with flecks and veins)
Height 7 mm; diameter 135 mm
India, probably Deccan, 17th century AD
Art market, 1994

8.12

8.12   OIL LAMP
LNS 356 HS
Carved from nephrite jade (very pale greenish grey,
    one side with russet mottling)
Height 45 mm; length 82; width at handles 80 mm
India, Deccan or Mughal, 17th century AD
Art market, 1998
Published: Sotheby's, London, 15 October 1998, 1, lot 134

8.13

8.13   SPITTOON
LNS 243 HS
Carved from nephrite jade (middle light green,
    with some black flecks)
Height 70 mm; length including handle 107; width 80 mm
India, Mughal or Deccan, 17th century AD
Art market, 1996
Published: Christie's, South Kensington, 27 June 1996, lot 257

8.14

8.14 KNIFE
LNS 84 I

Blade of *jawhar* steel; hilt carved from walrus ivory
   (eyes formerly inlaid)
Length 300 mm; max. width 40 mm
India, Mughal or Deccan, *c.* 1st half 17th century AD
Art market, 1997
Published: Sotheby's, London, 8 May 1997, lot 98

8.15 CRUTCH ('*ẒAFAR TAKĪYA*') HEAD
LNS 213 HS

Carved from nephrite jade (slightly variegated translucent light grey,
   with black flecks)
Height 75 mm; width 142 mm
India, Deccan or Mughal, *c.* 1st half 17th century AD
Art market, 1994

8.16 KNIFE
LNS 71 HS

Blade of *jawhar* steel, overlaid with gold; ferrule steel, overlaid with gold;
   hilt carved from nephrite jade (translucent pale greenish grey off-white)
Length 293 mm; width 39 mm
India, Deccan or Mughal, *c.* 1st half 17th century AD
Art market, 1991

8.16

8.17   DAGGER
LNS 70 HS

Blade of *jawhar* steel; hilt carved from nephrite jade
     (two pieces, both translucent white, the upper in
     particular absolutely pure)
Length 383 mm; width 96 mm
India, Deccan or Mughal, *c.* 1st half 17th century AD
Art market, 1991

8.18   DAGGER
LNS 172 HS

Blade of *jawhar* steel; hilt carved from nephrite jade
     (light greyish green), the eyes of rock crystal (painted details
     underneath); hilt inlaid with gold in *kundan* technique and
     set with rubies and an emerald at a later date
Length 373 mm; width 92 mm
India, Deccan or Mughal, *c.* 1st half 17th century AD
Art market, 1992

8.19   DAGGER
LNS 173 HS

Blade of *jawhar* steel; hilt carved from nephrite jade
     (two pieces, the top one ranging from dark grey,
     effectively black, to pale greenish grey off-white,
     the lower piece fairly uniform light grey); fitted
     with a fabricated gold halter at a later date
Length 385 mm; width 91 mm
India, Deccan or Mughal, *c.* 1st half 17th century AD
Art market, 1992

8.17

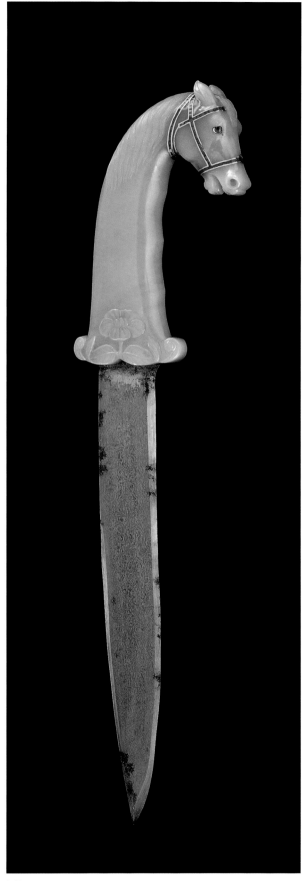

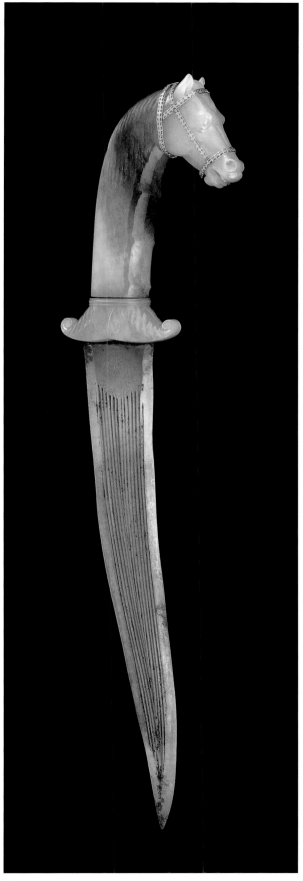

8.18

8.19

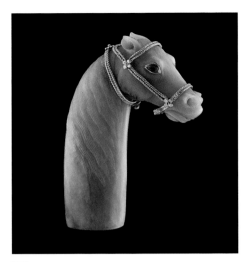

8.20

8.20   HILT
LNS 83 HS
Carved from nephrite jade (mottled pale greenish
    grey, with areas of tan and dark grey mottling);
    eyes inlaid with gold in *kundan* technique
    and set with rubies, and fitted with a gold
    halter fabricated from wire and shot,
    both at a later date
Length 69 mm; max. width 47 mm
India, Deccan or Mughal,
    c. 1st half 17th century AD
Art market, 1991

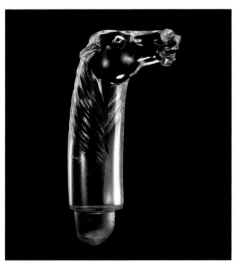

8.21

8.21   HILT
LNS 82 HS
Carved from rock crystal
Length 69 mm; max. width 34 mm
India, Deccan or Mughal,
    c. 1st half 17th century AD
Art market, 1991

8.22

8.22   HILT
LNS 50 HS
Carved from nephrite jade (pale green,
    with areas of whitish and tan mottling)
Length 118 mm; max. width 62 mm
India, Mughal or Deccan,
    c. 6th–7th decade 17th century AD
Art market, 1989

8.23 KNIFE
LNS 17 HS

Blade of *jawhar* steel overlaid with
gold; hilt carved from nephrite
jade (variegated greyish light
green, with cloudlike white areas
and one black stripe), inlaid with
gold in *kundan* technique and
set with rubies, chalcedony and
banded agate

Length 303 mm; max. width 46 mm

India, probably Deccan,
c. mid-17th century AD

Art market, 1980s

8.24 KNIFE
LNS 73 HS

Blade of *jawhar* steel; hilt carved
from nephrite jade (variegated
light to middle grey); eyes inlaid
with gold in *kundan* technique
and set with yellow sapphires
(painted details underneath)

Length 272 mm; max. width 43 mm

India, Deccan or Mughal,
2nd half 17th century AD

Art market, 1991

8.25 KNIFE
LNS 72 HS

Blade of *jawhar* steel overlaid with two
colours of gold; hilt carved from
nephrite jade (variegated pale and
darker grey, with white cloudlike
mottling and russet areas), eyes
inlaid with gold in *kundan*
technique and set with rubies
(at a later date?)

Length 275 mm; max. width 39 mm

India, Deccan or Mughal,
2nd half 17th century AD

Art market, 1991

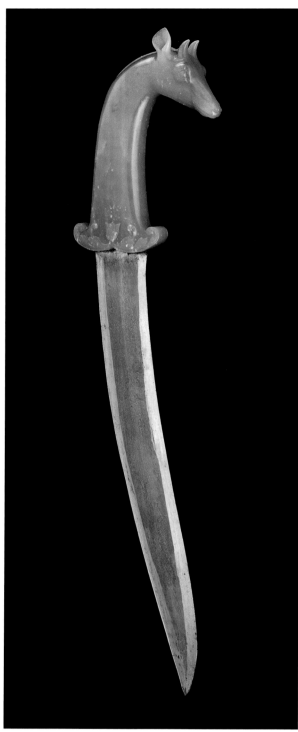

8.26

8.27

8.27   KNIFE
LNS 74 HS

Blade of *jawhar* steel, overlaid with gold; hilt carved
    from nephrite jade (two pieces, waxy middle green
    and pale grey off-white, respectively)
Length 206 mm; max. width 31 mm
India, Deccan or Mughal, 2nd half 17th century AD
Art market, 1991

8.26   DAGGER
LNS 81 HS

Blade of *jawhar* steel; hilt carved from nephrite jade (light green,
    with cloudlike white mottling and an area of black blotches)
Length 360 mm; max. width 88 mm
India, Deccan or Mughal, 2nd half 17th century AD
Art market, 1991

8.28   DAGGER
LNS 275 HS

Blade of *jawhar* steel; carved from nephrite jade (translucent
    slightly greenish palest grey off-white, with denser white flecks)
Length 358 mm; max. width 64 mm
India, Deccan (probably Hyderabad), mid–2nd half 17th century AD
Art market, 1997

8.28

8.29   CEREMONIAL MACE
LNS 354 HS
Carved from cryptocrystalline quartzes (variously patterned
and coloured agates, chalcedonies and jasper, the latter
bloodstone); with copper/copper-alloy dividers between
the sections, all threaded on an iron rod
Length 548 mm; max. diameter 76 mm
India, Mughal or Deccan, 17th century AD
Art market, 1998
Published: Christie's, London, 13 October 1998, lot 98

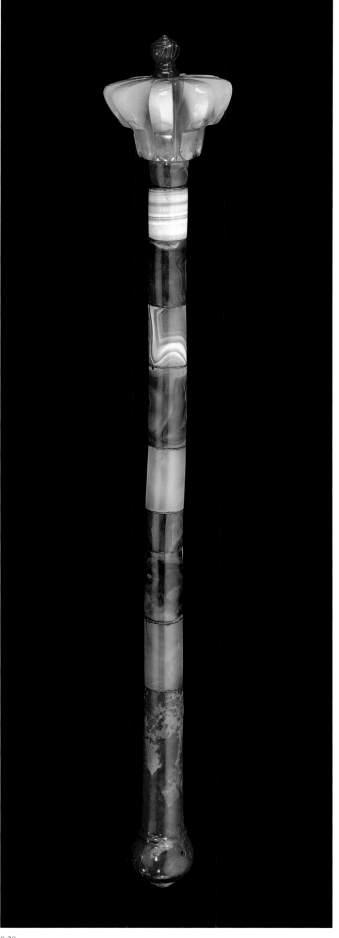

8.29

8.30

8.30   STANDARD

LNS 306 M

Fabricated from silver (hammered, worked in repoussé, engraved
and ringmatted, partially gilded); eyes inlaid with rock crystal
(painted details underneath)

Height of assembled pieces 505 mm;
length 502 mm; thickness 90 mm

India, probably Mughal (?), 17th century AD

Art market, 1991

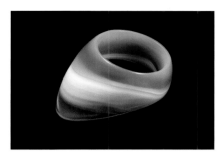

8.33

8.31

8.31 ARCHERY RING
LNS 2104 J
Carved from serpentine (dark green with paler green veins)
Height 17 mm; length 44 mm; width 29 mm
India, Mughal or Deccan, later 16th–17th century AD
Art market, 1998

8.33 ARCHERY RING
LNS 747 J
Carved from banded agate (translucent tan and white)
Height 20 mm; length 40 mm; width 29 mm
India, Mughal or Deccan, probably 1st half 17th century AD
Art market, 1992
Published: Sotheby's, London, 22 and 23 October 1992, lot 415

8.32

8.32 ARCHERY RING
LNS 367 HS
Carved from patterned agate (dark and light tan, and white)
Height 13 mm; length 44 mm; width 29 mm
India, Mughal or Deccan, probably 1st half 17th century AD
Art market, 1999
Published: Sotheby's, London, 22 April 1999, 2, lot 279

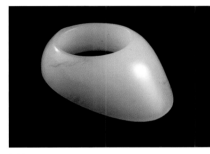

8.34

8.34 ARCHERY RING
LNS 2102 J
Carved from nephrite jade (white, with russet veins)
Height 18 mm; length 46 mm; width 34 mm
India, Deccan or Mughal, 17th century AD
Art market, 1992

8.35

8.35 ARCHERY RING
LNS 2103 J
Carved from nephrite jade (pale greyish green, with russet areas)
Height 16 mm; length 45 mm; width 31 mm
India, Deccan or Mughal, 17th century AD
Art market, 1992

8.36

8.37

8.36   FINGER RING WITH ROTATING AND BOBBING BIRD
LNS 751 J
Fabricated from gold, set in *kundan* technique with rubies,
    emeralds, chrysoberyl cat's eyes, diamonds and a
    single sapphire
Max. height 53 mm;
    width (with the bird oriented in the hole axis) 25 mm
India, Mughal or Deccan,
    probably *c.* 1st quarter 17th century AD
Art market, 1993

8.37   FINGER RING
LNS 752 J
Fabricated from gold, set in *kundan* technique
    with rubies, emeralds and turquoises
Height 50 mm; width 29 mm
India, Mughal or Deccan,
    probably *c.* 1st quarter 17th century AD
Art market, 1993

8.38   PENDANT
LNS 28 J
Fabricated from gold, front, head and neck worked in *kundan*
    technique and set with rubies, emeralds, diamonds and rock crystal;
    back engraved and inlaid with niello; with pendant pearls
Height excluding pendant elements 76 mm;
    width 55 mm; thickness 29 mm
India, probably Deccan, later 16th–1st quarter 17th century AD
Gift to the Collection, 1982
Published: Jenkins, Keene and Bates 1983, p. 133;
    Atil 1990, no. 98 (also in the French, Italian, German, Portuguese
    and Arabic editions); al-Qaddūmī 1996, fig. 8a and front cover

8.38

8.39

8.40

8.39 PENDANT
LNS 2217 J
Fabricated from gold, worked in *kundan* technique and
 set with rubies, emeralds, and a single diamond;
 with pendant pearls and emerald bead
Height excluding pendant elements 49 mm;
 width 33 mm; thickness 18 mm
India, Mughal or Deccan,
 c. 1st–2nd quarter 17th century AD
Art market, 1999
Published: Christie's, London, 6 October 1999, 2, lot 125

8.40 JEWELLED ELEMENT (MOUNT)
LNS 2003 J
Fabricated from gold, worked in *kundan* technique
 and set with rubies and emeralds
Height 39 mm; width 17 mm; thickness 12 mm
India, Mughal or Deccan, 17th century AD
Art market, 1998

8.41 ELEMENTS FROM A TURBAN ORNAMENT
LNS 91 HSa, b
Carved from emerald (fine middle green);
 eyes inlaid in *kundan* technique and set with rubies;
 mounted on enamelled gold, with silver staffs
Max. height 35 mm; average length 26 mm;
 average width 10 mm
India, Deccan or Mughal, probably 17th century AD
Art market, 1980s

8.41

9

RELIEF-CARVED ORNAMENT

SINCE ANCIENT TIMES, India has been the home of the world's most celebrated lapidary industry, and literary evidence from at least as early as the Greek and Roman eras attests to this renown. It is almost beyond doubt that, in antiquity and the medieval period, various at present unknown types of relief-carved hardstones would have been developed in the region, including both vessels (of agate, rock crystal, etc.) and precious gems. Unfortunately, no such objects are at this point known, although one may predict with reasonable confidence that examples will be identified in the future.

Fine hardstone relief carving from the early Islamic world is known in very considerable quantities, both in rock crystal and in the more abundant wheel-cut glass. Such schools would likely have benefited, variously, from Egyptian and Sasanian Persian (as well as Indian) traditions, with cross-fertilizations taking place as a result of the unifying effect of the early Islamic empire. Examples demonstrably of 10th-century East Iranian origin in the al-Sabah Collection show that, in addition to glass and rock-crystal vessels, extremely sophisticated and beautiful relief carving was also practised on gemstone jewelry elements. This tradition probably continued for some centuries beyond the period mentioned, and very possibly fed significantly into the Indian stream, particularly from the 12th century onward.

Whatever may be the details of the earlier medieval period's achievements, there is, from the latter part of the 16th-century onward, a remarkable series of Indian relief-carved emeralds of high levels of design and finish. On the material side, this was made possible by the importation of great quantities of large and marvellous emeralds from Colombia, newly available due to the extractions of the Spanish. These stones must have been carved in considerable numbers; but taking into account the fact that the intrinsic value of emerald is always a threat to the survival of historic stones (because of the great commercial temptation to recut those of fine quality), the al-Sabah Collection is fortunate to be able to present a glorious selection of this body of work here. The earliest firmly attributable piece which is known is the grand 233.5-carat, flat hexagonal stone with an asymmetrical design of swaying trees which has parallels

in the architectural decoration at the emperor Akbar's capital, Fatehpur Sikri (Cat. no. 9.1 [LNS 28 HS], probably carved *c.* 1575–85; although missing since the 1990 Iraqi invasion of Kuwait, photographs and records of it happily survive).

Other relief-carved emeralds shown here are more typical of the object-decorating arts of the period; they feature symmetrical designs which are nevertheless of subtle and lively execution, and are often expressive of the nature of the plant world which usually serves as the carvings' inspiration. These pieces also typically display to a marked degree precisely that formal beauty which guides their composition, and as such embody established canons of beauty found in most Islamic art.

The carved hardstone vessels, dagger hilts and other objects included here will be seen, in the character of their relief carving, to share much with the series of emeralds; and they have added interest in the manner in which the relief-carved elements relate to their overall form as functional objects, reinforcing the form artistically, and often structurally as well.

The layered agate cameo portrait of Shah Jahan, Cat. no. 9.11 (LNS 43 J), constitutes a special and particular case. Such controlled exploitation of thinly layered agates for decorative effect has an extremely ancient history in Western Asia and the Subcontinent, but the phenomenon as seen here obviously derives ultimately from classical portrait cameos. The artist clearly relied most importantly and directly on European Renaissance and Baroque examples (the latter representing a revival of the classical tradition), notwithstanding the fact that there was an awareness of ancient cameos in the immediately pre-Mughal Iranian and Indian contexts.

Although it has been repeatedly asserted that this piece (illustrated on page 114), as well as a comparable piece in the Victoria & Albert Museum, London, was carved by one of the European masters who found patronage in India, I take the position that the al-Sabah Collection's cameo in particular (the finer of the two) must have been carved by an Indian trained in the European tradition, since the drawing and rendering are entirely characteristic of the style of Indian artists, as abundantly evidenced in Mughal miniature paintings.

9.1

9.1   CENTREPIECE ELEMENT
LNS 28 HS

Carved from emerald (fine deep green), drilled

Height 50 mm; width 57 mm; thickness 10 mm; weight, 233.5 carats

India, Mughal, *c.* 8th–9th decade 16th century AD

Art market, 1982 (missing from the Collection as a consequence of the Iraqi invasion
of Kuwait in August 1990)

Published: Jenkins, Keene and Bates 1983, p. 124; Welch 1985, cat. no. 99; Swarup 1996, illus. 48

9.2

9.2 BORED EMERALD
LNS 2214 J

Carved from emerald (fine deep green, very slight
     bluish undertones), drilled
Height 31 mm; width 27 mm; thickness 15 mm;
     weight 90.4 carats
India, Deccan or Mughal, 16th–17th century AD
Art market, 1999
Published: Sotheby's, Geneva, 20 May 1998, lot 389

9.3

9.3 BORED EMERALD
LNS 35 HS

Carved from emerald (light green of great cleanness
     and 'water', slight bluish undertone), drilled
Height 37 mm; width 33 mm; thickness 12 mm;
     weight 110.1 carats
India, probably Mughal, *c.* 4th decade 17th century AD
Art market, 1980s
Published: Welch 1985, cat. no. 132; Pal et al. 1989, fig. 142

9.4

9.4 BORED EMERALD CENTREPIECE (OR BUTTON ?)
LNS 1817 J

Carved from emerald (fine deep green,
     bluish undertones), drilled
Diameter 18 mm; thickness 10 mm;
     weight 20.6 carats
India, Mughal or Deccan,
     later 16th–1st half 17th century AD
Art market, 1997

9.5

9.5 BORED EMERALD CENTREPIECE (OR BUTTON ?)
LNS 2196 J

Carved from emerald
     (fine deep middle green), drilled
Length 22 mm; width 18 mm;
     thickness 8 mm; weight 26.1 carats
India, Mughal or Deccan,
     later 16th–1st half 17th century AD
Art market, 1999

9.6

9.8

9.6 CENTREPIECE (NECKLACE OR UPPER ARMBAND, *BĀZŪBAND*)
LNS 2081 J
Carved from emerald (middle green), drilled
Length 37 mm; width at lugs 40 mm; thickness 15 mm;
    weight 187.2 carats
India, Mughal or Deccan, later 16th–1st half 17th century AD
Art market, 1998

9.8 CENTREPIECE (NECKLACE OR UPPER ARMBAND, *BĀZŪBAND*)
LNS 29 HS
Carved from emerald (deep green), drilled
Length 48 mm; width 33 mm; thickness 17 mm;
    weight 178.9 carats
India, Deccan or Mughal, *c.* 3rd quarter 17th century AD
Art market, 1981 (missing from the Collection as a consequence
    of the Iraqi invasion of Kuwait in August 1990)
Published: Jenkins, Keene and Bates 1983, p. 125

9.7

9.9

9.7 BORED EMERALD
LNS 90 HS
Carved from emerald (lightish green with bluish
    undertones), drilled
Length 41 mm; width 32 mm; thickness 26 mm;
    weight 235.0 carats
India, Deccan or Mughal,
    probably 1st half 17th century AD
Art market, 1991

9.9 PRINCIPAL DIVIDER FOR A STRAND OF PRAYER BEADS
LNS 97 HS
Carved from emerald (fine middle green,
    bluish undertones), drilled
Length 19 mm; diameter 12 mm; weight 16.9 carats
India, Deccan or Mughal,
    probably 1st half 17th century AD
Art market, 1992

9.10

9.11

9.11 PENDANT WITH CAMEO PORTRAIT OF THE EMPEROR SHAH JAHAN
LNS 43 J

Original part fabricated from gold, set in *kundan* technique with rubies and a cameo (layered agate, pinkish tan/white); the back fabricated from silver, engraved and inlaid with niello

Height including loop 37 mm; diameter 33 mm; thickness 8 mm

India: front Mughal, *c.* 6th decade 17th century AD; back Deccan (Hyderabad), 19th century AD

Art market, 1982

Published: Christie's, London, 7 December 1982, lot 88; Pal et al. 1989, fig. 137; Jellicoe 1990, pp. 14–15; Dehejia 1997, fig. 215

9.12

9.12 SEAL-RING (HOLOLITHIC) IN THE NAME OF AN OFFICER OF THE EMPEROR AWRANGZIB
LNS 121 J

Carved from nephrite jade (pale greyish green with subtle whitish flecks)

Height 27 mm; diameter of 'bezel' 30 mm

India, Mughal, with the date AH 1080 and the emperor Awrangzib's regnal year 12 (20 March–20 May AD 1670)

Art market, 1988

9.10 UPPER ARMBAND (*BĀZŪBAND*)
LNS 141 J

Fabricated from gold, champlevé-enamelled, set in *kundan* technique with a fine carved emerald (middle green), and other smaller emeralds (lightish, with coloured underlay) and diamonds

Length 90 mm; width including suspension loop 35 mm

Carved emerald India, probably Deccan, 2nd quarter 17th century AD; setting India, region uncertain, probably 19th century AD

Art market, 1979

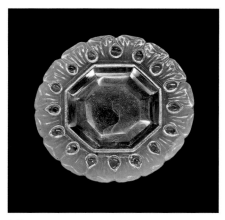

9.13

9.13   UPPER ARMBAND (*BĀZŪBAND*)
CENTREPIECE
LNS 1133 J
Carved from nephrite jade (light greyish green);
  inlaid with gold in *kundan* technique and set
  with rock crystal and rubies
Height 27 mm; diameter 56 mm
India, Deccan or Mughal,
  probably 1st half 17th century AD
Art market, 1994

9.14

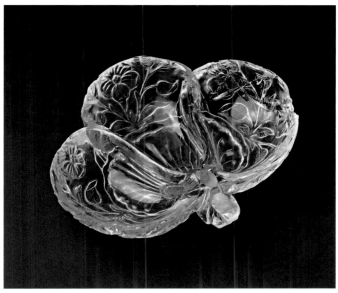

9.15

9.15   DISH
LNS 51 HS
Carved from rock crystal
Height 17 mm; length 59 mm; width 70 mm
India, Mughal, probably 2nd quarter 17th century AD
Art market, 1989

9.14   INKWELL
LNS 299 HS
Carved from nephrite jade (dark green with subtle variegations)
Height 63 mm; diameter 91 mm
India, Mughal, probably 4th quarter 16th century AD
Art market, 1998

9.16

9.17

9.17   POT (one handle missing)
LNS 66 HS
Carved from nephrite jade (variegated olive greenish grey
   with dark flecks and veins)
Height 71 mm; diameter of body 98 mm;
   width including handle 100 mm
India, Deccan or Mughal,
   probably 2nd–3rd quarter 17th century AD
Art market, 1991

9.16   KNIFE
LNS 365 HS
Blade steel, inlaid with gold; hilt carved from nephrite jade
   (pale green with tan areas)
Length 295 mm; max. diameter of hilt 23 mm
Hilt India, Mughal, probably 2nd quarter 17th century AD;
   blade dated AH 1215/AD 1800–1
Art market, 1999
Published: Christie's, London, 19 and 20 April 1999, lot 387

9.19

9.18

9.19 CUP
LNS 341 HS
Carved from nephrite jade (white of low translucency
with russet markings)
Height 18 mm; length 66 mm; width 43 mm
India, probably Deccan, 2nd–3rd quarter 17th century AD
Art market, 1998

9.18 POT
LNS 32 HS
Carved from nephrite jade (pale greyish green
with tiny black flecks)
Height 62 mm; diameter of body 93 mm;
width including handles 118 mm
India, Deccan or Mughal, 2nd–3rd quarter 17th century AD
Art market, 1980s

9.20

9.20 BOWL
LNS 322 HS
Carved from nephrite jade (pale greenish grey
with opaque areas on foot and one wall)
Height 54 mm; length 133 mm; width 107 mm
India, probably Deccan, 2nd–3rd quarter 17th century AD
Art market, 1998

9.21

9.21 DISH
LNS 320 HS

Carved from nephrite jade (light greyish green with whitish blotches)
Height 20 mm; diameter 175 mm
India, probably Deccan, 2nd–3rd quarter 17th century AD
Art market, 1998

9.22

9.22 CUP
LNS 327 HS

Carved from nephrite jade
(translucent off-white with whitish and tan areas)
Height 10 mm; length 82 mm; width 69 mm
India, probably Deccan, 2nd–3rd quarter 17th century AD
Art market, 1998

9.23

9.23 FINIAL (probably for a staff)
LNS 374 HS

Carved from patterned agate (layered dark
purplish grey, light yellowish grey and
milky whitish areas); fitted with a copper-
alloy ferrule for mounting on a shaft
Height including shaft 40 mm; diameter 41 mm
India, Mughal or Deccan,
later 16th–1st half 17th century AD
Art market, 1999
Published, Christie's, London, 12 October 1999, lot 122

9.24

9.24 CRUTCH ('*ẒAFAR TAKĪYA*') HEAD
LNS 343 HS

Carved from nephrite jade (three pieces variegated deep green
with bright green spots, two pieces translucent white);
set with foiled rock crystal at a later date, violating the ends
of the white jade buds
Height 48 mm; width 138 mm; thickness 25 mm
India, probably Deccan, *c.* 2nd quarter 17th century AD
Art market, 1998

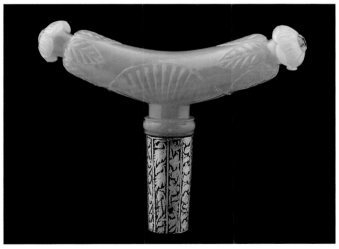

9.25

9.25 CRUTCH ('*ẒAFAR TAKĪYA*') HEAD
LNS 124 HS

Carved from nephrite jade (light slightly greyish green,
translucent and uniform); formerly inlaid with gold
and set with gemstones in *kundan* technique;
the steel ferrule overlaid with gold
Height 85 mm; width 114 mm; thickness 20 mm
India, probably Deccan, *c.* 2nd quarter 17th century AD
(ferrule later, probably 19th century AD)
Art market, 1992
Published: Sotheby's, London, 29 and 30 April 1992, lot 472

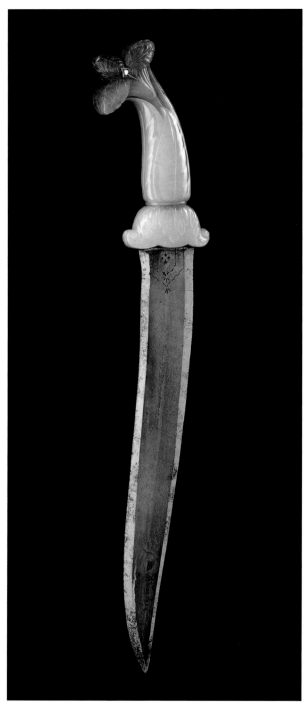

9.26

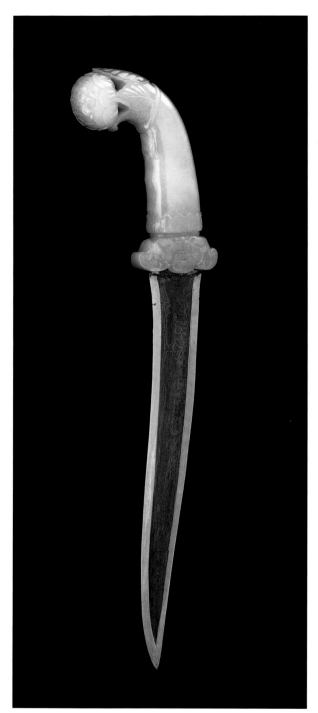

9.27

9.26   DAGGER
LNS 80 HS

Blade of *jawhar* steel; hilt carved from nephrite jade
   (quillons palest greyish off-white, grip and pommel blending
   from off-white to variegated grey with black flecks and russet
   marks); inlaid with gold in *kundan* technique and set with a
   ruby and diamonds at a later date

Length 395 mm; max. width 84 mm

India, Deccan, probably Hyderabad, *c.* 1st third 17th century AD

Art market, 1991

9.27   DAGGER WITH ORIGINAL LOCKET
LNS 174 HS

Blade of *jawhar* steel; hilt and locket carved from nephrite jade
   (translucent slightly greyish to greenish off-white, the former
   with russet staining in cracks, the latter with some white
   mottling)

Length 365 mm; max. width 90 mm

India, Deccan, probably Hyderabad, *c.* 1st third 17th century AD

Art market, 1992

9.29

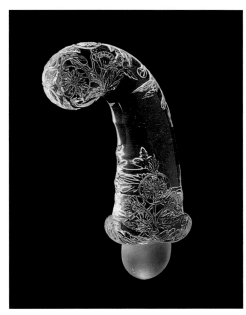

9.28

9.28   HILT (unfinished)
LNS 78 HS
Carved from rock crystal
Length 151 mm; max. width 85 mm;
    thickness 33 mm
India, Deccan (Hyderabad ?),
    c. 3rd–5th decade 17th century AD
Art market, 1991

9.29   DAGGER
LNS 79 HS
Blade of *jawhar* steel; hilt carved from nephrite jade
    (pale greyish green with some dark grey blotches)
Length 367 mm; max. width 68 mm
India, Deccan (Hyderabad ?),
    c. 3rd–5th decade 17th century AD
Art market, 1991

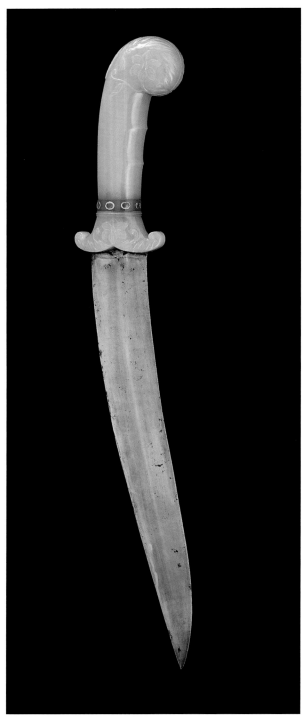

9.30

9.31

9.30   DAGGER
LNS 263 HS

Blade steel (repolished); hilt carved from nephrite jade
(three pieces: upper piece and quillons light greyish green,
band with rubies darker greyish green), inlaid with gold in
kundan technique and set with rubies

Length 380 mm; max. width 73 mm

India, Deccan (Hyderabad ?), *c.* 3rd–5th decade 17th century AD

Art market, 1997

9.31   DAGGER
LNS 264 HS

Blade of *jawhar* steel; hilt carved from nephrite jade
(variegated waxy middle green)

Length 388 mm; max. width 74 mm

India, Deccan (Hyderabad ?), *c.* 3rd–5th decade 17th century AD

Art market, 1997

9.32 DAGGER
LNS 253 HS

Blade of *jawhar* steel; hilt carved from nephrite jade
    (waxy middle green, one large dark-edged opaque blob)
Length 464 mm; max. width 76 mm
India, Deccan (Hyderabad ?), *c.* 3rd–5th decade 17th century AD
Art market, 1997
Ex coll.: The Sunde Collection, Copenhagen;
    and the Christensen Fund Collection, California
Published: Sotheby's, London, 8 May 1997, lot 56

9.33 DAGGER
LNS 252 HS

Blade of *jawhar* steel, overlaid and inlaid with gold; hilt carved
    from nephrite jade (pale green with russet-stained cracks)
Length 389 mm; max. width 100 mm
India, Deccan (Hyderabad ?), *c.* 4th–6th decade 17th century AD
Art market, 1997
Ex coll.: The Sunde Collection, Copenhagen;
    and the Christensen Fund Collection, California
Published: Sotheby's, London, 8 May 1997, lot 51

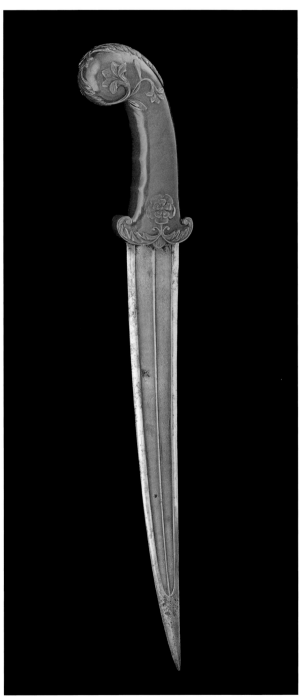

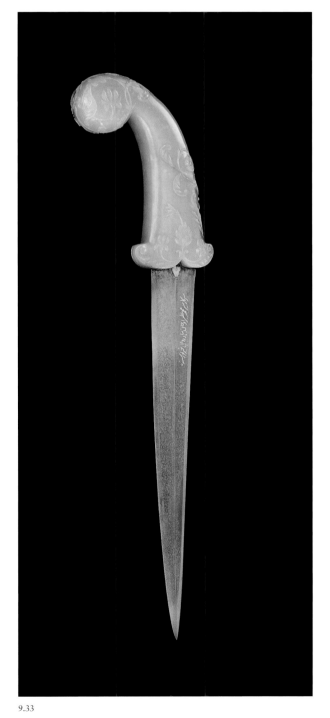

9.32

9.33

10

CARVED SET GEMSTONES

THIS SMALL GROUP has been set apart on account of the degree to which each piece features set stones which have their own individual interest because of the special forms into which they have been carved. This feature is also reasonably prominent in a number of other pieces which, however, have for various reasons been grouped under other headings (e.g., Cat. nos 1.4, 1.11, 2.29, 5.2, 5.3, 5.4, 5.6, 6.29, 6.43, 8.29, 8.36, 8.37, 8.38 and 13.22). All of these, along with related items in the al-Sabah and other collections, reinforce the attributions (to the earlier part of the Mughal era) which have been given to the pieces in this group.

In a wider sense, set stones carved in this fashion may be seen as part of an approach that encompasses cases such as those in which stones are purposely cut to form the edges of pieces, for example. All such approaches have their antecedents in ancient and medieval practice, but are pursued with particular distinction in the earlier part of the period with which we are concerned.

Especially noteworthy among the pieces here is the handle terminating in a dragon's head, Cat. no. 10.1 (LNS 1649 J), which is probably the upper part of the staff of a very high-ranking courtier. It is remarkable for its strongly salient crest, carved from ruby of superb quality; also notable are, for example, the cheeks, which are clad in, and the nose and eyebrows, which are carved from, rubies of similar excellence. These latter features are closely linked to such items as the dagger, Cat. no. 5.2 (LNS 25 J), and the bracelet clasp, Cat. no. 5.3 (LNS 208 J), again reinforcing interconnections between some of the finest extant Mughal-period jewelled objects.

Special attention should also be called to the fine ruby carvings of lions and feline masks on the upper side-bars of the grand *katar* dagger, Cat. no. 10.2 (LNS 163 J).

10.1

10.1   HANDLE (probably for a staff)
LNS 1649 J

Gold over an iron core, worked in *kundan* technique
    and set with rubies, emeralds, diamonds and agate
Length 101 mm; max. width 28 mm
India, Mughal or Deccan,
    late 16th–1st half 17th century AD
Art market, 1996

10.2   *KATAR* DAGGER AND SCABBARD
LNS 163 J

Blade of *jawhar* steel inlaid with gold; hilt and chape gold
    over an iron core, worked in *kundan* technique and set
    with rubies, emeralds and diamonds; locket gilded copper,
    worked in *kundan* technique and set with rubies, emeralds
    and a single diamond; scabbard wood, covered with red
    velvet with metal thread trimming
Length of dagger 450 mm; length in scabbard 487 mm;
    width 95 mm
India, Mughal or Deccan, *c.* 2nd quarter 17th century AD
Art market, 1989

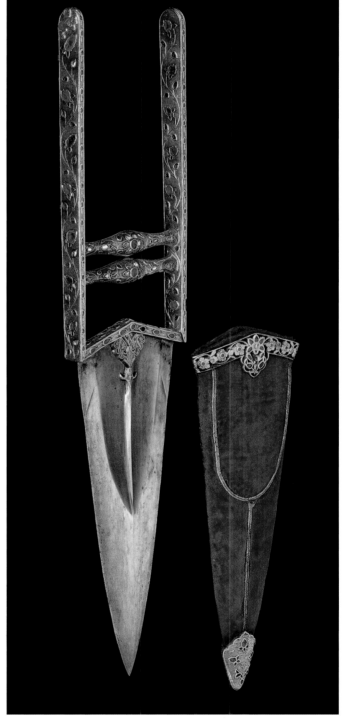

10.2

10.3

10.3   PENDANT
LNS 953 J

Fabricated from gold; with champlevé enamels;
worked in *kundan* technique and set
with rubies and emeralds; with pendant
emerald bead
Height excluding pendant emerald 38 mm;
height including pendant emerald 55 mm;
width 38 mm; thickness 7 mm
India, Deccan or Mughal,
c. 3rd–5th decade 17th century AD
Art market, 1993

10.4   LOCKET PENDANT
LNS 2034 Ja, b

Fabricated from gold, champlevé-enamelled, worked in *kundan*
technique and set with rubies and emeralds; with miniature
portrait by William Egley dated 1832, painted on ivory
covered with thin glass and fitted on a gold medallion
Height of locket including bail 82 mm;
height excluding bail, hinge and clasp 62 mm;
width 49 mm; thickness 11 mm;
diameter of medallion 44 mm
India, probably Deccan, *c.* 4th–5th decade 17th century AD
Art market, 1998
Published: Sotheby's, London, 24 April 1990, lot 171;
Bonhams, 29 April 1998, lot 211

10.4

10.5 DAGGER AND SCABBARD
LNS 115 J

Blade of *jawhar* steel; hilt, locket and chape carved
    from nephrite jade (the former very dark green,
    the latter two pale greenish grey off-white),
    all inlaid with gold in *kundan* technique
    and set with nephrite jade and rubies;
    scabbard wood covered with red fabric
    with metal thread trimming
Length of dagger 390 mm;
    length in scabbard 430 mm;
    max. width 100 mm
India, probably Deccan,
    c. 2nd quarter–mid-17th century AD
Art market, 1980s

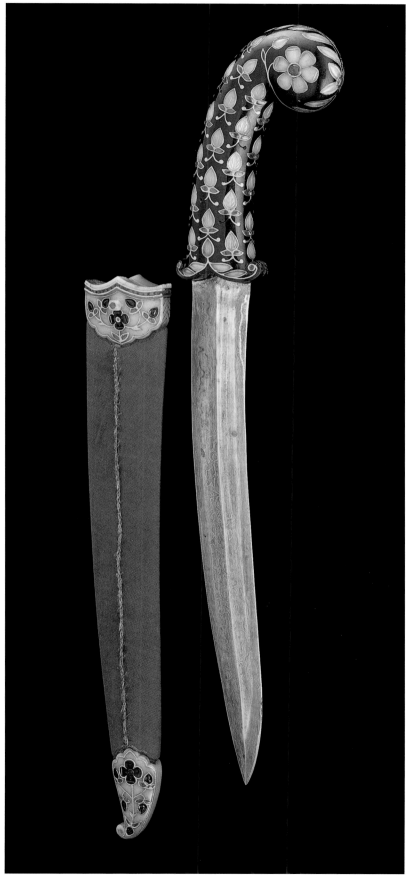

10.5

11

GEMSTONE FORMS

I T IS IMPORTANT FROM THE VERY OUTSET to have a clear understanding of the distinction between the treatment of precious and semi-precious stones in order to appreciate the variety and sophistication of the forms into which gemstones have been cut in the 'Orient'.

As a general rule, where precious stones are concerned, there has always been a strong natural disinclination to grind material away unnecessarily. As will be seen, this desire to avoid waste typically results in 'baroque' forms; but the cutters and grinders usually manage (while removing only areas with serious cracks or inclusions and giving an overall polish) to produce a form which is both pleasing and 'wearable'.

On the other hand, strict and skilful control of symmetry in the production of perfect, flat facets has been a feature of the cutting of semi-precious stones in Western Asia and the Subcontinent for thousands of years. Beads from Ur of the first half of the third millennium BC already exhibit such conceptions and expertise; and faceted beads from Taxila, especially of the period around the 1st century BC to the 1st century AD, afford a veritable encyclopaedia of beautiful and not infrequently quite complex polyhedral forms.

Similar interests and practice characterize artefacts from the medieval eastern Iranian world, where such forms also appeared in the shape of glass and bronze vessels, coin weights, and large beadlike fittings in a variety of materials. This tradition continued in various parts of the Islamic world into the late Middle Ages, with manifestations of it appearing in regions as widely separated as the Ottoman empire and the Deccan interior. One object included earlier, the elephant goad, Cat. no. 5.7 (LNS 314 M), demonstrates beyond doubt the living continuation of such types of cutting in India in the Mughal era. It must be stressed that this in no way indicates European influence: the forms and manner of execution constitute straightforward continuation of the region's tradition, stretching back through medieval Islamic practice to that of the Bactrian and Kushan periods (last centuries BC to first centuries AD).

Mughal miniature paintings occasionally provide evidence that even precious stones were sometimes cut into faceted forms which, again, represent indigenous tradition. One notable example (a miniature of Shah Jahan in the Freer Gallery of Art, Washington, D.C.) is extremely close in form to sizable numbers of early medieval eastern Iranian ringstones in rock crystal and similar materials (an important series of which is in the al-Sabah Collection).

Thus, the often-expressed notion that, before the 18th century, cutters in the East merely polished rough stones while retaining their irregular form (with the implication that they were not capable or in the habit of doing otherwise) is both erroneous and pernicious. The truth of the matter is that they had the requisite skills and practised them, their choice of form was conscious and deliberate, and they took advantage of a range of available options, whether the case called for a gemstone solid of high geometric interest, a glowing mass of glorious transparent gemstone colour, or something in between. This being the case, such forms as are seen in the beautiful pale-pink 'Golconda' diamond, Cat. no. 11.1 (LNS 2223 J), are placed in their true context. Here, the faceting is far from the most rigorous in the region's traditions, representing, as it does, a thoughtful and artistic compromise between retention of the size of the stone and enhancement of its brilliance.

Of ancient tradition and wholly characteristic is the quartz crystal–mimicking *taviz* (amulet) form into which two of the diamonds, Cat. nos 11.2 (LNS 1804 J) and 11.3 (LNS 2156 J), are cut. These are the most spectacular known exemplars (in terms of material, size and quality) of this traditional shape of Islamic and Indian stone pendants.

Also highly characteristic of tradition in India and the surrounding regions are the beads, made of the finest emerald; the large carved precious stones (see 'Relief-carved Ornament', pages 110ff.); and the small cups made from a single piece of gemstone. Notwithstanding the many literary references to the existence of these last, the examples presented here constitute extremely rare extant representatives of such types.

11.1

11.1 CUT STONE
LNS 2223 J

Facet-cut from diamond (material described as
'fancy light orange-pink')
Length 20 mm; width 16 mm; thickness 11 mm;
weight 24.8 carats
India, Deccan or Mughal, probably 17th century AD
Art market, 1999
Published: Christie's, London, 6 October 1999, 2,
lot 255

11.3

11.3 PENDANT OF *TAVIZ* (AMULET) OUTLINE
LNS 2156 J

Facet-cut from diamond (material described as 'fancy light pink'),
drilled
Height 33 mm; width 46 mm; thickness 3 mm; weight 56.7 carats
India, Deccan or Mughal, probably 17th century AD (or earlier)
Art market, 1999
Published: Jobbins, Harding and Scarrat 1984, pp. 1–7, figs 1–11;
Christie's, Geneva, 16 May 1985, lot 423;
Balfour 1987, pp. 41–43 (illus.);
Spink, London, 1988, no. 48;
Khalidi 1999, pp. 71–72

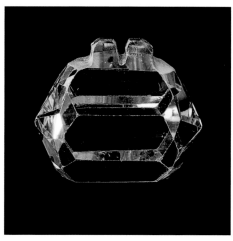

11.2

11.2 PENDANT OF *TAVIZ* (AMULET) FORM
LNS 1804 J

Facet-cut from diamond (material of yellowish tint),
drilled
Height 15 mm; width 17 mm; thickness 11 mm;
weight 28.3 carats
India, Deccan or Mughal, perhaps 17th century AD
(or earlier)
Art market, 1997

11.4

11.4   BEAD
LNS 2107 Jb
Cut from sapphire (fine middle blue), drilled
Length 29 mm; width 20 mm; thickness 18 mm;
    weight 106.6 carats
India, probably Mughal, *c.* later 16th–17th century AD
Art market, 1998
Published: Moses and Crowningshield 1997, p. 58, fig. 16

11.6

11.6   THREE BEADS
LNS 1765 Ja–c
Cut from spinel (fine purplish pink), drilled
(a) 24 × 15 × 11 mm, weight 22.1 carats
(b) 15 × 15 × 14 mm, weight 24.5 carats
(c) 16 × 14 × 12 mm, weight 23.5 carats
India, probably Mughal, *c.* later 16th–17th century AD
Art market, 1997

11.5

11.5   BEAD
LNS 2107 Jc
Cut from aquamarine (fine light greenish blue), drilled
Length 33 mm; width 24 mm; thickness 21 mm;
    weight 87.7 carats
India, probably Mughal, *c.* later 16th–17th century AD
Art market, 1998
Published: Moses and Crowningshield 1997, p. 58, fig. 16

11.7a

11.7a   STRAND OF BEADS
LNS 30 HS
Carved from emerald (fine deep green, several with slightly bluish
    undertones), drilled
Overall length of string 66 mm; length of largest bead 14 mm;
    diameter of largest bead 16 mm; length of smallest bead 2 mm;
    diameter of smallest bead 6 mm; overall weight 518.8 carats
India, Deccan or Mughal, *c.* later 16th–17th century AD
Art market, 1979
Published: Jenkins, Keene and Bates 1983, p. 131;
    Pal et al. 1989, fig. 141

11.7b

11.7b   BEAD
LNS 2371 Ja
Carved from emerald (fine green,
    with bluish undertones), drilled
Length 14 mm; diameter 14 mm;
    weight 22.6 carats
India, Deccan or Mughal,
    c. later 16th–17th century AD
Art market, 2000
Published: Sotheby's, St Moritz,
    16 and 17 February 2000, lot 514

11.8

11.8   CENTREPIECE (FOR A NECKLACE OR UPPER ARMBAND, *BĀZŪBAND*)
LNS 2224 J
Carved from emerald (fine deep middle green), drilled
Height 38 mm; width 43 mm; thickness 14 mm;
    weight 161.2 carats
India, Mughal or Deccan, later 16th–1st half 17th century AD
Art market, 1999
Published: Sotheby's, Geneva, 20 November 1991, lot 1024;
    Christie's, London, 6 October 1999, 2, lot 257

11.9   DAGGER
LNS 2194 J
Blade of *jawhar* steel; hilt carved from three pieces of emerald
    (green, with bluish undertones), drilled
Length with bail folded 380 mm; max. width 38 mm
Hilt India, probably Mughal, later 16th–early 17th century AD;
    ferrule and blade India, perhaps 18th century AD
Art market, 1999

11.9

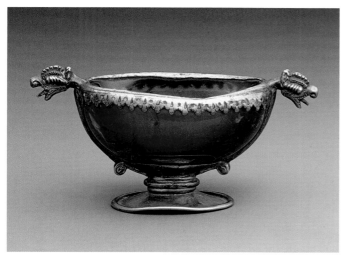

11.10

11.10 MINIATURE CUP
LNS 119 J

Carved from star garnet (deep reddish purple with brownish
    undertones, displaying asterism); with gilded silver mounts
Height 32 mm; length 64 mm; width 30 mm
India, probably Deccan, 16th century AD
Art market, 1988

11.11

11.11 MINIATURE CUP, INSCRIBED WITH
PERSIAN VERSES
LNS 22 HS

Carved from emerald (retaining the crystal form, upper part green
    with bluish undertones, blending to opaque material at the
    base); wheel-cut inscription
Height 41 mm; max. width between faces 38 mm;
    max. width between corners 43 mm; weight 252.0 carats
India, Deccan or Mughal, later 16th–17th century AD
Art market, 1980s
Published: al-Qaddūmī 1996, fig. 3b

12

INSCRIBED ROYAL GEMSTONES

ROYAL INSCRIPTIONS APPEAR on gemstones already in the third millennium BC in Mesopotamia. Of the known ancient examples, most seem to date from the second millennium BC, the stones mainly being fancy agates, but also including, for example, blue chalcedony and turquoise.

Not so fundamentally different in character, yet constituting a distinct (and much later) set of inscribed royal gemstones, are an impressive and important series, the great majority of which are engraved with the names of Mughal emperors. This was, however, a practice inherited by the Mughals from their ancestors, the Timurids, who in turn continued a tradition known among the Mongol emperors as far back as the 13th century AD. The earliest record of this line of practice at present known to art-historical scholarship suggests that the rulers of Badakhshan may have been its originators at some point in or before the 13th century AD. Since their territory included the mines of 'balas rubies' (red gem spinels, on which by far the greatest number of extant royal inscriptions occur), and since these rulers were reputed to have been a very ancient line, a certain plausibility attaches to this suggestion.

The earliest-known extant example of such an inscription, by more than one hundred years, is that of the Timurid Ulugh Beg (died 1449) on Cat. no. 12.1 (LNS 1660 J). This stone also features the unique instance of such an inscription in the name of a Safavid ruler (Shah Abbas I). Additionally, it bears the names of three Mughal emperors (Jahangir, Shah Jahan and Awrangzib) and of the Afghan king Ahmad Shah. This stone has been famous in literature since before it was sent to Jahangir by Shah Abbas I, and is the very stone fabled in recent literature as the 'Timur Ruby'.

The al-Sabah Collection includes not only this incomparably important Timurid stone, but its holdings in the area of royally inscribed spinels are by a vast margin the largest in the world, with the exception only of the National Jewels Treasury (the former Crown Jewels) of Iran. And it is also characteristic of the al-Sabah Collection that the second-oldest such inscription known is to be found on another of its spinels, Cat. no. 12.2 (LNS 2107 Ja).

A limited number of emeralds and diamonds so inscribed show that such inscriptions were not confined to spinels. The Mughals, as well as at least one Deccani ruler and the Persian conqueror Nadir Shah, are all represented by inscriptions on diamonds. One can only suspect that the intrinsic value of the material in the case of diamonds and emeralds (and thus the impulse to recut them) has led to their extremely low survival rate. Conversely, historic spinels (and all of us whose interest they excite) have proven fortunate precisely because of the low per-carat market value of this material in relatively recent times.

Two other inscribed gemstones of the Mughal period included under this heading carry inscriptions which represent another category which, while religious in content, may also be fairly described as 'royal', because of the practically certain princely status of the patron. These are the superb emeralds, Cat. nos 12.24 (LNS 36 HS) and 12.25 (LNS 1766 J), exquisitely inscribed with the Throne Verse from the Qur'an. Like those in the names of Mughal rulers, these inscriptions were executed with a diamond-tipped stylus (as opposed to being wheel-cut, which was the practice for sealstones), which afforded particularly great control of the process. When many times magnified, the calligraphy can be seen to embody artistically faultless proportions, on a par with the monumental architectural inscriptions of the period – an exalted standard indeed.

12.1

12.2

**12.1   INSCRIBED ROYAL SPINEL ('BALAS RUBY')
LNS 1660 J**

Cut from spinel (fine slightly purplish deep pink, with a soft, 'velvety' quality),
    drilled, manually engraved with a diamond stylus, and wheel-cut
Length 48 mm; width 36 mm; thickness 18 mm; weight 249.3 carats
Inscriptions:
    (1) Timurid, Ulugh Beg (before AD 1449)
    (2) Safavid, Shah Abbas I (dated AH 1026/AD 1617)
    (3) Mughal, Jahangir (dated AH 1030/AD 1621)
    (4) Mughal, Shah Jahan (undated)
    (5) Mughal, Alamgir [Awrangzib] (dated AH 1070/AD 1659–60)
    (6) Durrani, Ahmad Shah (dated AH 1168/AD 1754–55)
Art market, 1996

**12.2   INSCRIBED ROYAL SPINEL
('BALAS RUBY') BEAD   LNS 2107 Ja**

Cut from spinel (very fine reddish pink with
    purplish undertones); drilled and manually
    engraved with a diamond stylus
Length 33 mm; width 25 mm; thickness 19 mm;
    weight 114.4 carats
Inscriptions:
    (1) Mughal, Akbar (dated AH 971/1563–64 AD)
    (2) Mughal, Jahangir (undated)
    (3) Mughal, Shah Jahan (dated AH 1038 and
    regnal year 1/AD 1628–29)
Art market, 1998
Published: Moses and Crowningshield 1997,
    p. 58, figs 16 and 17

12.5–12.19

12.3

12.3 INSCRIBED ROYAL SPINEL ('BALAS RUBY') BEAD
LNS 2222 Ja

Cut from spinel (slightly purplish deep pink);
  drilled and manually engraved with a
  diamond stylus
Length 20 mm; width 16 mm; thickness 10 mm;
  weight 25.4 carats
Inscriptions:
  (1) Mughal ('*La'l Jalāli*' ['Glorious Spinel'/'Spinel of Jalāl'],
  probably reign of Akbar, referring to his title 'Jalāl ad-Dīn')
  (2) Mughal, Jahangir (dated AH 1018/AD 1609–10)
Art market, 1999
Published: Christie's, London, 6 October 1999, 2, lot 253

12.4

12.4 INSCRIBED ROYAL SPINEL ('BALAS RUBY') BEAD
LNS XXV SH

Cut from spinel (fine slightly purplish pink);
  drilled and manually engraved with a
  diamond stylus
Length 23 mm; width 23 mm; thickness 11 mm;
  weight unknown, perhaps *c*. 60 carats
Inscription: Mughal, Jahangir (dated AH 1015/AD 1606–7)
Art market, 1980s (missing from the Collection as a
  consequence of the Iraqi invasion of Kuwait in August 1990)

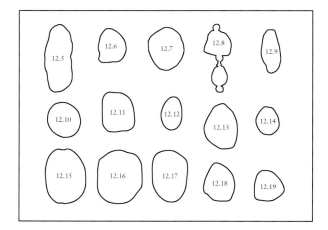

12.5   INSCRIBED ROYAL SPINEL ('BALAS RUBY') BEAD
LNS 1757 J

Cut from spinel (deep purplish pink);
    drilled and manually engraved with a diamond stylus
Length 40 mm; width 16 mm; thickness 14 mm;
    weight 70.6 carats
Inscriptions:
    (1) Mughal, Jahangir (dated AH 1015/AD 1606–7)
    (2) Mughal, Shah Jahan (dated AH 1039 and regnal
    year 2/AD 1629–30)
Art market, 1997

12.6   INSCRIBED ROYAL SPINEL ('BALAS RUBY') BEAD
LNS 1758 J

Cut from spinel (fine purplish pink);
    drilled and manually engraved with a diamond stylus
Length 18 mm; width 18 mm; thickness 10 mm;
    weight 29.9 carats
Inscription: Mughal, Jahangir (dated AH 1016/AD 1607–8)
Art market, 1997

12.7   INSCRIBED ROYAL SPINEL ('BALAS RUBY') BEAD
LNS 1759 J

Cut from spinel (fine purplish pink);
    drilled and manually engraved with a diamond stylus
Length 25 mm; width 21 mm; thickness 14 mm;
    weight 57.1 carats
Inscription: Mughal, Jahangir (dated AH 1017/AD 1608–9)
Art market, 1997

12.8   INSCRIBED ROYAL SPINEL ('BALAS RUBY') BEAD
WITH PENDANT PEARL
LNS 2140 J

Cut from spinel (fine purplish pink);
    drilled and manually engraved with a diamond stylus;
    threaded with a gold wire with pendant pearl and green
    glass bead
Length of stone 13 mm; width 16 mm; thickness 11 mm;
    'height' including wire and pearl 42 mm;
    weight with wire and pearl 32.5 carats
Inscription: Mughal, Jahangir (dated AH 1017/AD 1608–9)
Art market, 1998

12.9   INSCRIBED ROYAL SPINEL ('BALAS RUBY') BEAD
LNS 1760 J

Cut from spinel (fine deep purplish pink);
    drilled and manually engraved with a diamond stylus
Length 26 mm; width 13 mm; thickness 10 mm;
    weight 24.2 carats
Inscriptions:
    (1) Mughal, Jahangir (dated AH 1017/AD 1608–9)
    (2) Mughal, Shah Jahan (dated AH 1049 and regnal
    year 12/AD 1639–40)
Art market, 1997

12.10   INSCRIBED ROYAL SPINEL ('BALAS RUBY') BEAD
LNS 2093 J

Cut from spinel (deep purplish pink);
    drilled and manually engraved with a diamond stylus
Length 21 mm; width 20 mm; thickness 12 mm;
    weight 45.6 carats
Inscription: Mughal, Jahangir (dated AH 1018/AD 1609–10)
Art market, 1998

12.11   INSCRIBED ROYAL SPINEL ('BALAS RUBY') BEAD
LNS 1740 J

Cut from spinel (high pink with purplish undertones);
    drilled and manually engraved with a diamond stylus
Length 24 mm; width 19 mm; thickness 9 mm;
    weight 40.9 carats
Inscription: Mughal, Jahangir (dated AH 1018/AD 1609–10)
Art market, 1997

**12.12 INSCRIBED ROYAL SPINEL ('BALAS RUBY') BEAD
LNS 1761 J**

Cut from spinel (purplish pink);
    drilled and manually engraved with a diamond stylus
Length 20 mm; width 13 mm; thickness 11 mm;
    weight 27.2 carats
Inscription: Mughal, Jahangir (dated AH 1020/AD 1611–12)
Art market, 1997

**12.13 INSCRIBED ROYAL SPINEL ('BALAS RUBY') BEAD
LNS 46 HS**

Cut from spinel (purplish pink, areas of heavy inclusions);
    drilled and manually engraved with a diamond stylus
Length 30 mm; width 19 mm; thickness 17 mm;
    weight 77.5 carats
Inscriptions:
    (1) Mughal, Jahangir (undated)
    (2) Mughal, Shah Jahan (dated AH 1043 and regnal
    year 6/AD 1633–34)
Art market, 1980s
Published: Keene 1984, no. 35

**12.14 INSCRIBED ROYAL SPINEL ('BALAS RUBY') BEAD
LNS 55 HS**

Cut from spinel (fine deep purplish pink);
    drilled and manually engraved with a diamond stylus
Length 17 mm; width 14 mm; thickness 10 mm;
    weight 20.3 carats
Inscription: Mughal, Jahangir (last two digits of date absent
    due to repolishing)
Art market, 1980s

**12.15 INSCRIBED ROYAL SPINEL ('BALAS RUBY') BEAD
LNS 123 Jb**

Cut from spinel (fine red-purple);
    drilled and manually engraved with a diamond stylus
Length 33 mm; width 23 mm; thickness 17 mm;
    weight 121.3 carats
Inscriptions:
    (1) Mughal (?) ('*Muḥammad Rasūl Allāh*'
    ['Muḥammad is the Prophet of God'])
    (2) Mughal, Jahangir (formerly dated AH 1018/AD 1609–10,
    this date and other parts of the inscription now lost due to
    repolishing)
    (3) Mughal, Shah Jahan (any date lost due to repolishing)
Art market, 1986
Published: Stronge 1996, fig. 4 (right stone)

**12.16 INSCRIBED ROYAL SPINEL ('BALAS RUBY') BEAD
LNS 123 Ja**

Cut from spinel (fine red-purple); drilled and wheel-cut
Length 32 mm; width 28 mm; thickness 23 mm;
    weight 186.1 carats
Inscriptions:
    (1) Mughal, Jahangir or Shah Jahan
    (almost entirely obliterated due to repolishing)
    (2) Durrani, Ahmad Shah (dated AH 1168/AD 1754–55)
Art market, 1986
Published: Stronge 1996, fig. 4 (central stone)

**12.17 INSCRIBED ROYAL SPINEL ('BALAS RUBY') BEAD
LNS 123 Jc**

Cut from spinel (fine red-purple);
    drilled and manually engraved with a diamond stylus
Length 31 mm; width 20 mm; thickness 22 mm;
    weight 113.3 carats
Inscriptions:
    (1) Mughal, Jahangir (any date lost due to repolishing)
    (2) Mughal (? undeciphered, considerable loss due to
    repolishing)
Art market, 1986
Published: Stronge 1996, fig. 4 (left stone)

**12.18 INSCRIBED ROYAL SPINEL ('BALAS RUBY') BEAD
LNS 1763 J**

Cut from spinel (fine deep purplish pink);
    drilled and manually engraved with a diamond stylus
Length 25 mm; width 19 mm; thickness 14 mm;
    weight 49.5 carats
Inscriptions:
    (1) Mughal, Jahangir (any date lost due to repolishing)
    (2) Mughal, Shah Jahan (any date lost due to repolishing)
Art market, 1997

**12.19 INSCRIBED ROYAL SPINEL ('BALAS RUBY') BEAD
LNS 1764 J**

Cut from spinel (fine purplish pink);
    drilled and manually engraved with a diamond stylus
Length 20 mm; width 16 mm; thickness 14 mm;
    weight 36.0 carats
Inscription: Mughal, Jahangir (any date lost due to repolishing)
Art market, 1997

12.20

12.20 INSCRIBED ROYAL SPINEL ('BALAS RUBY') BEAD
LNS 1762 J

Cut from spinel (fine purplish pink);
    drilled and manually engraved with a diamond stylus
Length 21 mm; width 17 mm; thickness 12 mm; weight 35.6 carats
Inscription: Mughal, Shah Jahan (dated AH 1045/AD 1635–36)
Art market, 1997

12.21

12.21 INSCRIBED ROYAL SPINEL
('BALAS RUBY') BEAD FRAGMENT
LNS 1153 J

Cut from spinel (purplish pink material
    of uncertain saturation); drilled and
    manually engraved with a diamond
    stylus (subsequently sawn off the
    stone on which it appeared)
Length 7 mm; width 8 mm;
    thickness 4 mm; weight 2.3 carats
Inscription: Mughal, Shah Jahan
    (dated AH 1049/AD 1639–40)
Art market, 1994

12.22

12.22 INSCRIBED ROYAL SPINEL ('BALAS RUBY') BEAD
LNS 57 HS

Cut from spinel (fine deep red-purple);
    drilled and manually engraved with a diamond stylus
Length 44 mm; width 28 mm; thickness 24 mm;
    weight 245.9 carats
Inscriptions:
    (1) Mughal, Shah Jahan (any date lost due to repolishing)
    (2) Mughal (uncertain but later date, recording its gift from
        Shah Jahan to an unspecified person)
Art market, 1989

12.24

12.24   CENTREPIECE, INSCRIBED WITH THE THRONE VERSE FROM THE QUR'AN (II:255)
LNS 36 HS

Cut from emerald (exceptionally superb rich deep green, of
   excellent cleanness); manually engraved with a diamond stylus
Height 35 mm; width 31 mm; thickness 8 mm; weight 73.2 carats
India, Mughal or Deccan, 17th century AD
Art market, 1982 (missing from the Collection as a consequence of
   the Iraqi invasion of Kuwait in August 1990)

12.23

12.23   INSCRIBED ROYAL EMERALD
LNS 2173 J

Cut from emerald (rich middle green, of great
   cleanness and 'water'); inscription wheel-cut;
   the stone recently recut
Length 27 mm; width 18 mm; thickness 13 mm;
   weight 59.6 carats
Inscription: Afsharid, Nadir Shah
   (dated AH 1153/AD 1740–41 – stone probably
   taken from the Mughal Royal Treasury in
   1739), recut in the 20th century, leaving
   the inscription largely intact
Art market, 1999

12.25

12.25   CENTREPIECE, INSCRIBED WITH THE THRONE VERSE FROM THE QUR'AN (II:255)
LNS 1766 J

Cut from emerald (rich middle green, of excellent cleanness);
   manually engraved with a diamond stylus
Height 29 mm; width 34 mm; thickness 10 mm; weight 85.6 carats
India, Mughal or Deccan, 17th century AD
Art market, 1997

13
JEWELLED MAGNIFICENCE

IN THE END, all the tools, skills, materials and absorbed traditions at the disposal of the artist are nothing more than that, except for the degree to which he employs them to embody his visions in successful pieces. Those in the present grouping have no special theme of association except for their high celebration of precious stones and their embodiment of the Indian jeweller's insufficiently celebrated genius for orchestrating multifarious and inherently seductive elements into an entirely digestible, quintessentially artistic whole. This factor of the elements' individually engrossing character, and certainly also their own intrinsic value, are potentially inhibitory to their use in an imaginative manner in which they are allowed to exhibit their glory while being under the artistic control necessary to a unified and harmonious production.

As we have seen, the material shown and described in this catalogue largely comes from the earlier part of the Mughal era. Most of the pieces included under this heading also derive from that period, but also constitute perhaps a slightly higher proportion of later examples than elsewhere. To the degree that this is so, they amply demonstrate the artists' continuing high standards, even though later taste may have evolved in directions that are less appealing to us than is the case with the earlier pieces.

Although there remains some demand for traditional types of jewelry, ensuring a certain survival (if at a low ebb) of the old skills and traditions, the context which produced the marvels shown and described here has vanished. One can only attribute causes of the demise of the 'Mughal period style' (and a myriad other co-existent traditional types of India) to the overwash of a certain version of European culture and taste, no less powerful for being accompanied chronologically by the rejection and overthrow of European political control. A new synthesis and vital development in this art, as in so many others of our day, would best thrive in an atmosphere of enlightened patronage, ecumenical openness, general curiosity and cultural excitement of the type that characterized the Mughal era at its most creative.

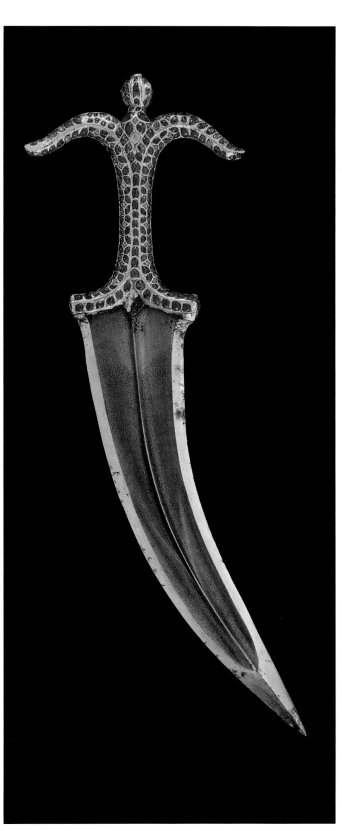

13.1   DAGGER
LNS 113 J

Blade of *jawhar* steel; hilt iron overlaid with gold, worked in
kundan technique and set with rubies, turquoises and
emeralds; scabbard wood overlaid with red velvet with metal
thread trimming; chape gold, worked in *kundan* technique,
and set with rubies and emeralds

Length of dagger 342 mm; max. width 105 mm

India, Mughal, late 16th–earlier 17th century AD

Art market, 1980s (missing as a consequence of the Iraqi invasion
of Kuwait in August 1990; recognized at auction in London
[see below], graciously withdrawn from the sale and returned
to the Collection)

Published: Sotheby's, London, 17 October 1996, lot 46

13.2   DISH
LNS 1785 J

Fabricated from gold, worked in *kundan* technique
and set with rubies and emeralds

Height 9 mm; diameter 100 mm

India, Mughal, *c.* 1st quarter 17th century AD

Art market, 1997

Published: Sotheby's, London, 8 May 1997, lot 141

13.1

13.2

13.4 a–d FOUR BOXES
LNS 2163 J LNS 2164 J
LNS 2165 J LNS 2166 J
Fabricated from gold, worked in *kundan* technique,
    each set with rubies, emeralds and a diamond
Average height 35 mm; average diameter 43 mm
India, Deccan or Mughal,
    c. 2nd–3rd quarter 17th century AD
Art market, 1999

13.3   CASE FOR A CEREMONIAL CONCH SHELL
LNS XXXV SH
Fabricated from gold, worked in *kundan* technique and set
    with rubies, emeralds, diamonds and chrysoberyl cat's eyes
Length 170 mm; width including loops 80 mm; thickness 64 mm
India, probably Deccan, *c.* 3rd–5th decade 17th century AD
Art market, 1970s
Published: Zebrowski 1997, 1, pl. 45

13.3

13.4a–d

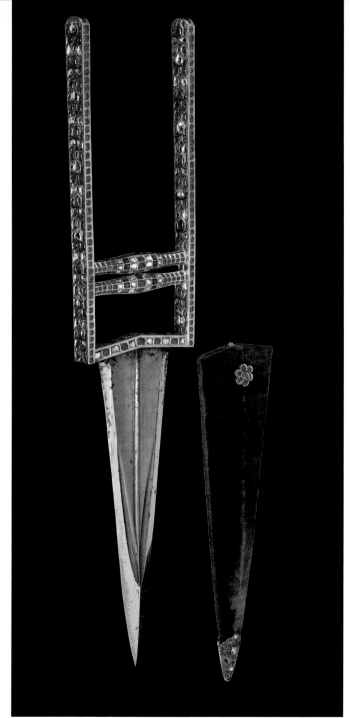

13.5

13.6

13.5 *KATAR* DAGGER WITH SCABBARD
AND LOCKET
LNS 114 J

Blade of *jawhar* steel (repolished), overlaid with gold; hilt gold over
an iron core, worked in *kundan* technique and set with rubies,
emeralds and diamonds; scabbard wood covered with red silk
and green velvet; locket fabricated from gold, worked in
kundan technique and set with rubies, emeralds and diamonds

Length of dagger 355 mm; length in scabbard 375 mm;
width 102 mm

India, Mughal, *c.* 2nd quarter 17th century AD

Art market, 1980s

Published: Pal et al. 1989, fig. 172

13.6 *KATAR* DAGGER WITH SCABBARD
AND CHAPE
LNS 214 J

Blade of *jawhar* steel; hilt gold over an iron core, worked in
kundan technique and set with rubies, emeralds and diamonds;
scabbard wood overlaid with green velvet and metal thread
trimming; locket and chape fabricated from gold, worked in
kundan technique and set with rubies, emeralds and diamonds

Length 448 mm; length in scabbard 472 mm; width 98 mm

India, Mughal, *c.* 2nd quarter 17th century AD

Art market, 1991

13.7 *KATAR* DAGGER
LNS 211 J

Blade of *jawhar* steel; hilt gold over an iron core;
worked in *kundan* technique and set with rubies,
emeralds and diamonds; engraved

Length 374 mm; width 90 mm

India, Mughal, *c.* 2nd quarter 17th century AD

Art market, 1991

Published: Atil 1997, no. 99 (also in the Arabic edition)

13.8 *KATAR* DAGGER
LNS 117 J

Blade of *jawhar* steel (repolished); hilt gold over an iron core,
worked in *kundan* technique and set with rubies, emeralds
and diamonds; engraved

Length 385 mm; width 93 mm

India, Mughal, *c.* 2nd quarter 17th century AD

Art market, 1989

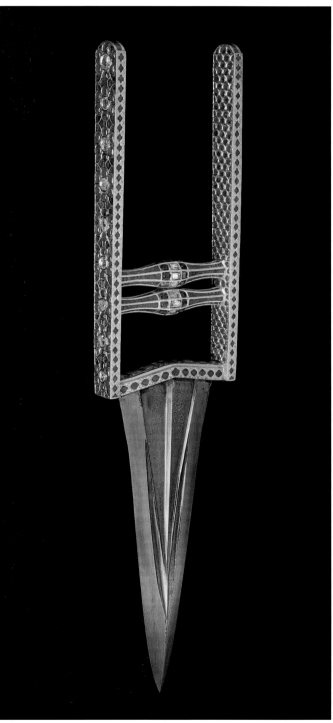

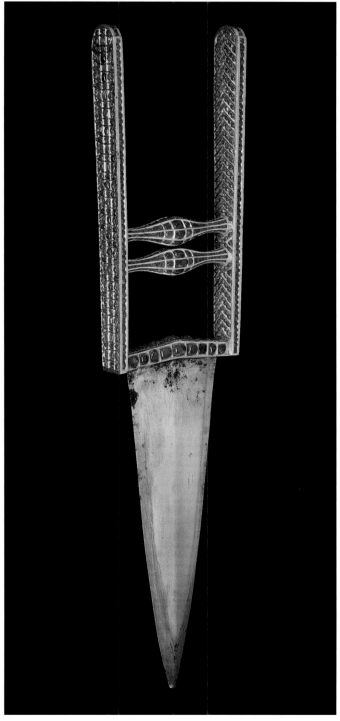

13.7

13.8

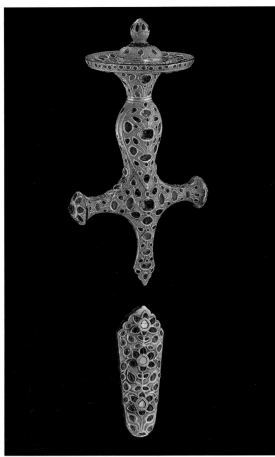

13.9

13.9   SWORD HILT AND CHAPE
LNS 126 Ja, b

Hilt and chape gold over an iron core, ringmatted and worked
    in *kundan* technique; the former set with rubies and
    emeralds, the latter with rubies, emeralds and diamonds
Length of hilt 168 mm; width at quillons 93 mm;
    diameter of disc 66 mm; length of chape 81 mm;
    width 29 mm
India, probably Mughal, *c.* 2nd–3rd quarter 17th century AD
Art market, 1986

13.10   DAGGER AND SCABBARD WITH ORIGINAL
LOCKET AND CHAPE
LNS 212 Ja, b

Blade of *jawhar* steel overlaid with gold; hilt gold over an iron
    core, worked in *kundan* technique and set with rubies,
    emeralds and diamonds; scabbard wood overlaid with silk
    woven in floral designs, with metal thread trimming;
    locket and chape fabricated from gold, worked in *kundan*
    technique and set with rubies, emeralds and diamonds
Length of dagger 373 mm; length in scabbard 410 mm;
    max. width 82 mm
India, Deccan or Mughal, *c.* 3rd quarter 17th century AD
Art market, 1991
Published: Atil 1997, no. 100 (also in the Arabic edition)

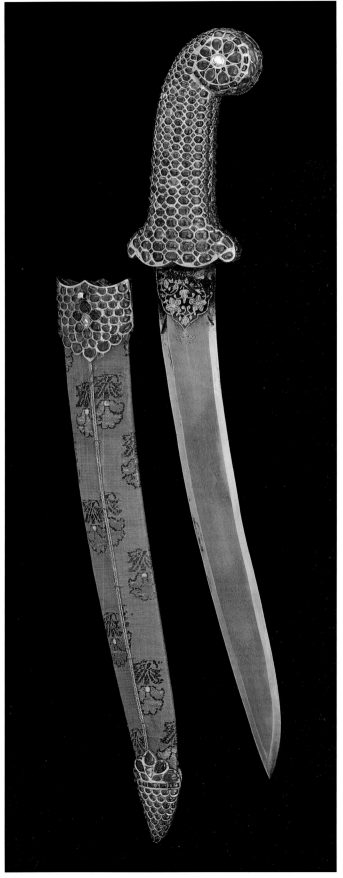

13.10

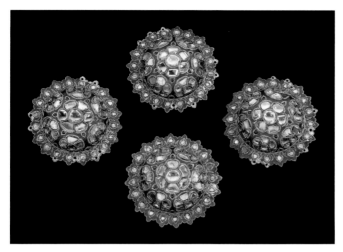

13.11

13.11 SET OF SHIELD BOSSES
LNS 209 Ja–d

Fabricated from gold, champlevé-enamelled, worked in *kundan* technique
    and set with diamonds and emeralds
Average height 21 mm; average diameter 57 mm
India, Deccan or Mughal, *c.* 2nd–3rd quarter 17th century AD
Art market, 1991

13.12

13.12 SET OF SHIELD BOSSES
LNS 1865 Ja–d

Fabricated from gold, worked in *kundan* technique and set with
    rubies, diamonds and emeralds; central attachment post capped
    with champlevé enamel
Average height including pin 29 mm; average diameter 57 mm
India, Deccan or Mughal, *c.* 2nd–3rd quarter 17th century AD
Art market, 1997
Published: Christie's, London, 8 October 1997, lot 350

13.13

13.13 GROUP OF SHIELD BOSSES
LNS 1819 Ja–c

Fabricated from gold, champlevé-enamelled, worked in
    kundan technique and set with diamonds and emeralds
Measurements (height, width, thickness), bottom to top:
    (a) 82 × 93 × 11 mm; (b) 69 × 75 × 9 mm;
    (c) 57 × 67 × 6 mm
India, Deccan or Mughal, *c.* 3rd quarter 17th century AD
Art market, 1997

13.14

13.14 PENDANT
LNS 1129 J

Fabricated from gold, worked in *kundan* technique
   and set with diamonds, rubies and emeralds;
   with pendant pearl
Height excluding pendant pearl 23 mm;
   height including pendant pearl 33 mm;
   width 19 mm; thickness 4 mm
India, probably Mughal,
   c. 2nd–3rd decade 17th century AD
Art market, 1994

13.15 PAIR OF BRACELETS
LNS 1206 Ja, b

Fabricated from gold, worked in *kundan* technique
   and set with rubies and emeralds
Average diameter 69 mm;
   average thickness of shank top to bottom 13 mm;
   average width of shank excluding clasp 15 mm
India, Deccan or Mughal,
   c. 3rd–4th quarter 17th century AD
Art market, 1991

13.15

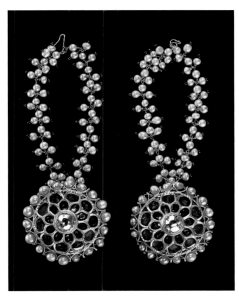

13.17

13.16

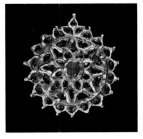

13.18

13.16   PAIR OF EARPLUGS WITH ATTACHMENT BAND
LNS 1815 J
Fabricated from gold, champlevé-enamelled, worked in *kundan* technique
   and set with emeralds and diamonds; with strung and pendant pearls
(As illustrated) height including hook 244 mm; width 183 mm;
   average height of earplugs including pendant elements 68 mm;
   average width of earplugs 29 mm; average thickness of earplugs 19 mm
India, Deccan or Mughal, *c.* 3rd–4th quarter 17th century AD
Art market, 1997

13.17   PAIR OF EARPLUGS
LNS 1810 Ja, b
Fabricated from gold, worked in *kundan*
   technique and set with diamonds,
   emeralds and rubies; with strung and
   pendant pearls
Average diameter of earplugs 43 mm;
   average thickness of earplugs 19 mm;
   average length of strings of pearls
   including hooks 88 mm
India, Deccan or Mughal, *c.* 3rd–4th
   quarter 17th century AD
Art market, 1997

13.18   EARPLUG
LNS 290 J
Fabricated from gold, worked in
   kundan technique and set with
   diamonds, rubies and emeralds
Height including loop 43 mm;
   width 39 mm; thickness 13 mm
India, Deccan or Mughal, *c.* 3rd–4th
   quarter 17th century AD
Art market, 1980s

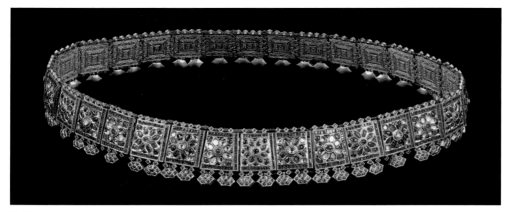

13.19

13.19   BELT
LNS 160 J

Fabricated from gold; worked in *kundan* technique
and set with diamonds, rubies and emeralds;
backs of units matrix-stamped
(As illustrated) max. dimensions at upper edge
of belt: depth 240 mm; width 380 mm;
max. dimensions at lower edge of belt:
depth 380 mm; width 415 mm; average height of
single segment including pendant elements 58 mm;
average thickness of segments 12 mm
India, Deccan or Mughal,
probably *c.* 1st half 18th century AD
Art market, 1980s

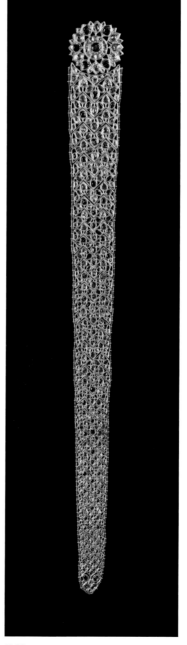

13.20   HAIR-PLAIT ORNAMENT
LNS 161 J

Fabricated from gold, worked in *kundan* technique
and set with diamonds, rubies and emeralds
Height 555 mm; width 52 mm
India, Deccan or Mughal, *c.* 18th century AD
Art market, 1980s

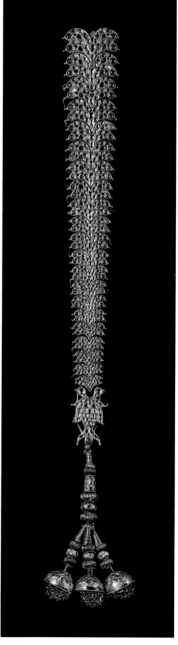

13.21   HAIR-PLAIT ORNAMENT
LNS 177 J

Fabricated from gold; worked in *kundan* technique
and set with diamonds, rubies and emeralds;
back of fish repoussé-worked; pendant elements
champlevé-enamelled
Height 553 mm; width 53 mm
India, Deccan or Mughal, *c.* 18th century AD
Art market, 1980s

13.20   13.21

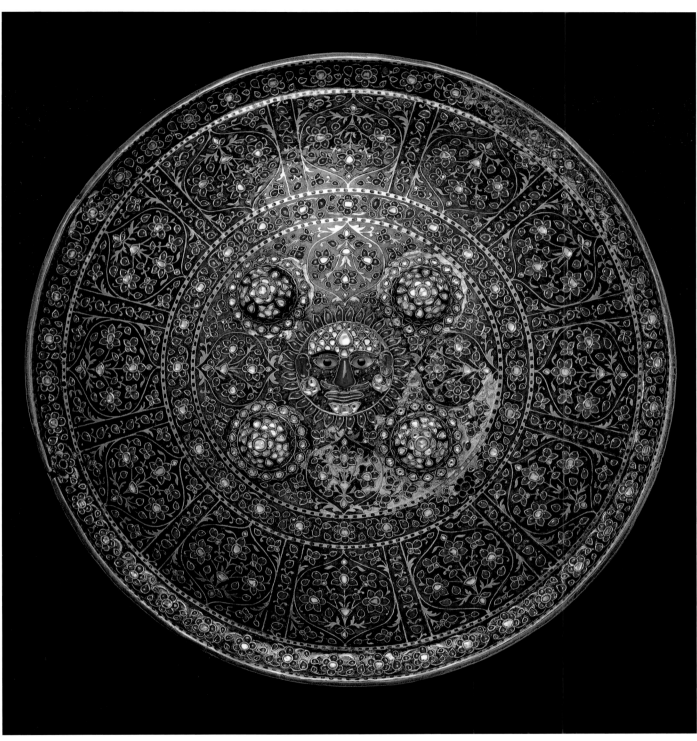

13.22

13.22 SHIELD
LNS 2162 J
Hammered up from silver sheet, champlevé-enamelled and gilded,
    set in *kundan* technique with rubies, diamonds, emeralds,
    chalcedony, agate and rock crystal
Diameter 488 mm; thickness 75 mm
India (probably Central or North), *c.* 18th century AD
Art market, 1999

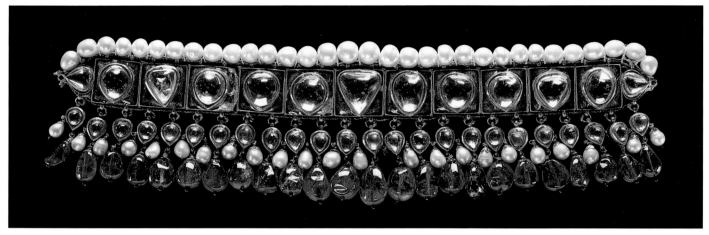

13.23

13.23 CHOKER NECKLACE
LNS 9 J

Fabricated from gold; worked in
kundan technique and set with
diamonds; with champlevé enamels;
strung with pearls and with pendant
emerald beads and pearls
Height 81 mm; length 282 mm
India, probably Deccan (Hyderabad),
18th–19th century AD
Art market, 1979

13.24 PAIR OF ANKLETS
LNS 1813 Ja, b

Fabricated from gold, champlevé-
enamelled, worked in *kundan*
technique and set with diamonds
and a single ruby (the latter in
centre of diamond on 'a')
Max. dimension 120 mm;
thickness 25 mm
India, Deccan,
19th–earlier 20th century AD
Art market, 1997

13.24

GLOSSARY

AH
Anno Hegirae, or Hijra year, indicating the universal Islamic system of dating, which counts from the year of the flight, or *hijra*, of the Prophet Muhammad from Mecca to Madina (AD 622).

ANKUSH or ELEPHANT GOAD
Short staff terminated by two blades, one of which is a straight extension of the axis, the other radically curved through 180 degrees. This is a classically Indian implement of ancient origin, used by the mahout, or elephant driver, to control and direct the animal.

ARCHERY RING
Ring worn by an archer on the thumb of the release hand, increasing control and affording protection from the bruising power of the bowstring. In the period here concerned, it is prolonged on one side, to protect the entire ball of the thumb, which holds the bowstring in the Oriental or 'Mongolian' release.

ASTERISM
The effect which produces 'stars' (hence the name) in precious stones. Typically, this is caused by reflection off long fibres of another material, such as rutile, inside the stone; as these are present in large numbers and are precisely oriented in different axes, the reflection of light off them causes the appearance of a 'star' which moves across the 'surface' of the stone as light angles change.

BAIL
Jewelry element which functions like the bail of a bucket, providing a suspension point while preserving desirable movement by some type of swivelling or swinging arrangement.

BALAS RUBY (RED SPINEL)
A distinct species of precious stone much in favour in the medieval and later periods from the Subcontinent and China through western Europe. As 'true', or corundum, rubies were not available in very large sizes, this was the most attractive red stone available to fill the need.

BAROQUE
A term used to refer to a stone or a pearl which is of an irregular, rounded, 'lumpy' form.

BASSE-TAILLE ENAMELS
Type in which low relief is executed in the metal and subsequently covered by transparent enamels, the relief thus seen through the enamel forming an integral part of the design.

BĀZŪBAND
Type of upper armband with an ancient history in India, in which a relatively thin element encircles the arm just below the shoulder to display on the outer surface of the upper arm a jewel or jewelled creation.

BEZEL
Term used to refer to the configuration which holds the stone of a ring and, by extension, to the entire upper part thereof. Also used to refer to the sloping facets which flank the 'table' of a cut stone.

CAMEO
A carving which takes advantage of the decorative potential of different levels in a material which has contrastingly coloured layers.

CHAMPLEVÉ ENAMELS
'Lifted field' enamels, i.e., those in which the areas to be filled with enamel are excavated with gravers and chisels, rather than having applied elements such as wire or metal strips to separate the colours.

CHANNEL SETTING
A type much in evidence in the pieces presented here, in which small stones are abutted in line, without transverse gold bands separating them, but held only by the gold at the sides.

CHAPE
The lower fitting which terminates, gives definition to and ornaments a sword or dagger scabbard. The examples catalogued here are of materials ranging from gold-inlaid iron and enamelled gold to gem-set gold and jade.

CHASE
To decoratively tool a surface with punches, chisels, etc. Usually signifies an action in which little material is removed, in contrast with engraving.

CLOISONS
Cell walls, usually made of metal strips, which are applied to the surface of a jewelled item, creating compartments (for stones, enamels, etc.) and dividing elements of the design.

COLLET SETTING (i.e., 'SIMPLE COLLET SETTING')
Type of setting in which a simple ring, usually formed of an edge-set strip of metal, holds the stone.

DAGGER SASH-CORD
Cord which secures the scabbard and prevents it and the dagger from slipping or being jostled out of the sash (inside which daggers were invariably carried in the Mughal period).

DAGGER SASH-CORD ORNAMENT
As here encountered, usually of jade. When in the form of a 'medallion' (i.e., circular) it is carved with a pair of lugs on the back for threading on to the cord (see immediately above), to appear ornamentally at the waist. Another popular form of sash-cord ornament is domical, and acts as 'ferrule' to a 'tassel', either of gold threads or of small pearls.

DAMASCENING (see OVERLAID STEEL; also INLAID STEEL)

DEVANAGARI SCRIPT
The most commonly encountered script used for rendering Indian languages in the Mughal period, aside from the Arabic/Persian. *Devanagari* was (and is) used to write Sanskrit, as well as regional languages, over vast swaths of the Subcontinent.

DUCTILITY
As used here, the degree of ability of a metal to be drawn out into a longer and thinner form, which largely comes into play in the making of wire by drawing it through successively smaller holes in a drawplate; gold is the most ductile of metals (see MALLEABILITY).

FINIAL
Decorative element which terminates an artistic entity, from architecture to the tiniest portable objects.

FOILED SETTING
Type in which thin metal foil, often artificially coloured, is placed under a transparent stone for reflectance and/or colour. Normally encountered when the setting is closed, the stone receiving no light except through the top.

HOLOLITHIC
Used to refer to an object, such as a finger ring, which is made entirely of stone (typically one piece), whereas such objects are normally made of, for example, metal, and set with stones.

HUQQA (HOOKAH)
Term (of Arabic origin) most often used here for the reservoir for liquid (most commonly water) through which smoke is filtered to render it cooler, milder and less injurious.

INCLUSIONS
(in the interiors of precious stones). Refers to tiny, most often microscopic, bodies, cavities, etc., which are of different material from that of the stone itself.

INLAID STEEL
The ornamentation of steel with precious metals (usually gold) which are beaten or pressed into areas previously excavated. This is most commonly of a linear character, but at times is more expansive.

INLAY
Used variously here as a noun to refer to that which is inlaid into some article, and as a verb to refer to the setting of precious metals into excavated depressions in an object, the latter usually of hardstone or steel.

JAWHAR STEEL
The term used in Arabic and Persian to refer to what is ordinarily called 'Damascus' steel, which is characterized by swirling patterns of hard and soft zones within the steel, and which appears on the surface of a forged, ground and polished object as wavy 'watered' patterns after a light etch in a mild acid.

KATAR DAGGER
A uniquely Indian type, the most fundamental peculiarity of which is a grip in the form of cross-bars, allowing the heel of the palm to apply the full strength of the arm to the thrust. The second essential of the design is the side-bars, which parallel the forearm and add the needed control and guidance, as well as a certain amount of protection.

KUNDAN WORK
Uniquely Indian technique of joining hyper-purified gold, in the form of foil, through pressure alone, to form a molecular bond at room temperature. This obviates soldering, allowing working procedures, types of construction and the joining of materials in ways which would be otherwise impossible, greatly empowering the jeweller to realize his visions.

LOCKET
The upper fitting which terminates, reinforces, protects, gives definition to and ornaments a sword or dagger scabbard. In the case of a sword scabbard, it often incorporates lugs, bails, etc., for the attachment of suspension straps; and in the daggers involved here, it often incorporates a lug for a cord which secures the dagger in the sash (see DAGGER SASH-CORD and DAGGER SASH-CORD ORNAMENT).

LUG
As used here, an integral element, usually pierced, for suspension or for the attachment of one object to another via cords, BAILS (which see), etc.

MALLEABILITY
As used here, the degree of ability of a metal to be successfully beaten or stretched out into a form with larger surface area, becoming thinner in the process (see DUCTILITY).

MATTED
Used to refer to a surface which has been given a matte, or non-shiny, textured surface, especially through treatment by a rough-ended tool driven by light hammer-blows.

NIELLO
Black substance which is fired into or on to the surface of a precious metal, in a manner analogous to enamelling. Niello is variously composed of silver, copper, lead and sulphur, which are first melted and quenched, then ground up, applied and fired, like the ground-up glass used for enamels.

OVERLAID STEEL
The type most commonly referred to by the unfortunate and much-abused term 'Damascening/Damascene work'. In this, the area to be ornamented is hatched with a sharp chisel to raise burrs, which are bent over and grip the precious metal when the latter is hammered on to them.

OVERLAY
Used variously here as a noun to refer to the gold or silver which is overlaid into some article of metal, and as a verb to refer to the hammering-on of precious metals.

PATINATED
Condition of a metal surface which has been permanently coloured for decorative value. This may be achieved with various chemicals or, as in the case of steels, by controlled heating.

PAVÉ
'Paved', a modern kind of setting in which small stones are so closely set that little of the metal of which the piece is made remains visible.

POMMEL
The termination, usually some sort of swelling, at the end of a dagger or sword hilt; ultimately from Latin *pomellum*, 'little apple', the form of which was approximated by the pommels of a number of types of European hilts.

QUILLONS
The arms of the cross-guard of a sword or dagger.

REPOUSSÉ WORK
Classically, sheet metal which is hammered up, mostly from the back side, into relief. As encountered here, not normally in fact 'repoussé' at all, being entirely worked from the front, usually against a bed of pitch.

RICASSO
The part of a blade immediately adjacent to the hilt; often lavishly decorated in princely Indian daggers.

RINGMATTED
Describes a metal surface which has been given an all-over small-figure texture by a hammer-driven chisel with circular configurations with voided centres in its end, producing tiny depressed circles or 'rings'.

SPINEL (see BALAS RUBY)

SUBSTRATE
The body or substantial element upon which other elements are placed, into which they are inlaid, etc.

TAVIZ
From Arabic *ta'wīdh*, 'charm', 'amulet'. As encountered here, a type of pendant horizontally oriented, hollow and with a removable end for the insertion of protective texts, etc.; also used for pendants of similar form, even when cut from hardstones.

TORQUE
Used here to designate a rigid necklace, whether cast, forged or of heavy twisted wire. This is a very ancient and widespread type, with a long history in the Subcontinent.

WATER, WATERED, WATERING (see *JAWHAR* STEEL)

ẒAFAR TAKĪYA
A type of crutch which was popular in India and often made of luxurious and artistically worked materials. These were most often short, for use while sitting or reclining on floor mats/cushions, and sometimes contained, inside the shaft, a stiletto-like blade.

ZAR-NISHĀN
Term used in Mughal India to refer to those whose work was to inlay precious metals, especially gold, into the likes of steel and hardstones, having cut channels and/or fields below the surface to receive and grip the precious metal.

BIBLIOGRAPHY

WORKS CITED IN ABBREVIATED FORM IN THE CATALOGUE

Amsterdam 1990
> *Time-Life History of the World: The European Emergence*
> AD *1500–1600*, Amsterdam, 1990

Atil 1990 [Atil 1994] [Atil 1997]
> Atil, Esin, ed., *Islamic Art and Patronage: Treasures from Kuwait*,
> New York, 1990 (also editions in French [1992], Italian [1994],
> German [1996], Portuguese [1997] and Arabic [1999])

Atil, Chase and Jett 1985
> Atil, Esin; Chase, W. T.; and Jett, Paul, *Islamic Metalwork in the*
> *Freer Gallery of Art*, Washington, D.C., 1985

Balfour 1987
> Balfour, Ian, *Famous Diamonds*, London, 1987

Bloom and Blair 1997
> Bloom, Jonathan, and Blair, Sheila, *Islamic Arts*, London, 1997

Bonhams, 29 April 1998
> *Islamic Works of Art*, Bonhams, Knightsbridge (London),
> Wednesday 29th April 1998

Bonhams, 14 October 1998
> *Islamic Works of Art*, Bonhams, Knightsbridge (London),
> Wednesday 14th October 1998

Bonhams, 13 and 14 October 1999
> *Islamic Works of Art*, Bonhams, Knightsbridge (London),
> Wednesday 13th and Thursday 14th October 1999

Christie's, Geneva, 16 May 1985
> *A Spectacular Historic Table-cut Diamond*, Christie's, Geneva,
> Thursday May 16th, 1985

Christie's, London, 7 December 1982
> *Antique Jewellery, including A Collection of Cameos*, Christie's,
> London, Tuesday 7 December 1982

Christie's, London, 18 and 20 October 1994
> *Islamic Art, Indian Miniatures, Rugs and Carpets*, Christie's,
> London, Tuesday 18 and Thursday 20 October 1994

Christie's, London, 3 July 1996
> *Works of Art from The Bute Collection*, Christie's, London, 3 July 1996

Christie's, London, 8 October 1997
> *Important Indian Jewellery*, Christie's, London, Wednesday 8 October 1997

Christie's, London, 14 October 1997
> *Islamic Art and Indian Miniatures*, Christie's, London,
> Tuesday 14 October 1997

Christie's, London, 28 April 1998
> *Islamic Art and Indian Miniatures*, Christie's, London,
> Tuesday 28 April 1998

Christie's, London, 13 October 1998
> *Islamic Art and Manuscripts*, Christie's, London,
> Tuesday 13 October 1998

Christie's, London, 19 and 20 April 1999
> *Islamic Art, Manuscripts and Printed Books of Iranian Interest*,
> Christie's, London, Monday 19 April and Tuesday 20 April 1999

Christie's, London, 6 October 1999, 2
> *Magnificent Mughal Jewels*, Christie's, London,
> Wednesday 6 October 1999

Christie's, London, 12 October 1999
> *Islamic, Indian and Armenian Art and Manuscripts*, Christie's, London,
> Tuesday 12 October 1999

Christie's, South Kensington, 27 June 1996
> *Oriental Ceramics and Works of Art*, Christie's, South Kensington
> (London), 27 June 1996

Christie's, South Kensington, 7 October 1997
> *Indian Jewellery*, Christie's, South Kensington (London),
> 7 October 1997

Dehejia 1997
> Dehejia, Vidya, *Indian Art*, London, 1997

Habsburg, Feldman, Geneva, 29 June 1988
> *Antique Jewellery, Miniatures, Objects of Vertu, Fabergé, Russian*
> *and Islamic Works of Art*, Habsburg, Feldman, Hôtel des Bergues,
> Geneva, Wednesday, June 29, 1988

Habsburg, Feldman, Geneva, 14 May 1990
> *Gold: Important Ancient and Ethnic Jewellery and Works of Art in*
> *Precious Metal*, Habsburg, Feldman, Hôtel des Bergues, Geneva,
> 14 May, 1990

Habsburg, Feldman, New York, 25 October 1989
> *Fine Islamic, Persian and Indian Works of Art*, Habsburg, Feldman,
> New York, October 25, 1989

Jellicoe 1990
> Jellicoe, Patricia, 'A Moveable Feast of Mughal Romance',
> in *Eastern Art Report*, vol. 11, no. 2 (June 1990)

Jenkins, Keene and Bates 1983
> Jenkins, Marilyn (ed.); Keene, Manuel; and Bates, Michael,
> *Islamic Art in the Kuwait National Museum: The al-Sabah Collection*,
> London, 1983

Jobbins, Harding and Scarrat 1984
> Jobbins, E. A.; Harding, R. R.; and Scarratt, K., 'A Brief Description
> of a Spectacular 56.71 Carat Tabular Diamond', in *The Journal of*
> *Gemmology*, vol. XIX, no. 1 (January 1984)

Keene 1984
> Keene, Manuel (with contributions and translation into Arabic by Ghada
> Hijjawi Qaddumi), *Dar al-Athar al-Islamiya, Kuwait National Museum:*
> *Selected Recent Acquisitions*, Kuwait, AH 1404 /AD 1984

Khalidi 1999
> Khalidi, Omar, *Romance of the Golconda Diamonds*, Middletown,
> New Jersey, 1999

Leoshko 1988
> Leoshko, Janice, 'Romance of the Taj Mahal', in *Marg*,
> vol. XLI, no. 2 (1988)

Moses and Crowningshield 1997
> Moses, Thomas, and Crowningshield, G. Robert, 'Mogul Talismans',
> in *Gems & Gemology*, vol. 33, no. 1 (Spring 1997)

Pal et al. 1989
> Pal, Pratapaditya; Leoshko, Janice; Dye, Joseph M. III; and Markel, Stephen, *Romance of the Taj Mahal*, Los Angeles and London, 1989

Qaddumi 1987
> Qaddumi, Ghada Hijjawi, *Variety in Unity: A Special Exhibition on the Occasion of the Fifth Islamic Summit in Kuwait*, Kuwait, 1987

al-Qaddūmī 1996
> al-Qaddūmī, Ghāda al-Ḥijjāwī, trans. and annot., *Book of Gifts and Rarities (Kitāb al-Hadāyā wa al-Tuḥaf), Selections Compiled in the Fifteenth Century from an Eleventh-Century Manuscript on Gifts and Treasures*, Cambridge, Massachusetts, 1996

Sotheby's, Geneva, 20 November 1991
> *Important Indian Jewellery*, Sotheby's, Geneva, Wednesday 20 November 1991

Sotheby's, Geneva, 20 May 1998
> *Magnificent Jewels*, Sotheby's, Geneva, Wednesday 20 May 1998

Sotheby's, London, 24 April 1990
> *Indian, Himalayan and South-East Asian Art*, Sotheby's, London, Tuesday 24th April 1990

Sotheby's, London, 24 and 25 April 1991
> *Islamic and Indian Art*, Sotheby's, London, 24th and 25th April 1991

Sotheby's, London, 29 and 30 April 1992
> *Islamic and Indian Art, Oriental Manuscripts and Miniatures*, Sotheby's, London, 29th and 30th April 1992

Sotheby's, London, 22 and 23 October 1992
> *Islamic and Indian Art, Oriental Manuscripts and Miniatures*, Sotheby's, London, 22nd and 23rd October 1992

Sotheby's, London, 21 October 1993
> *Himalayan, Indian and South-East Asian Art*, Sotheby's, London, Thursday 21 October 1993

Sotheby's, London, 27 April 1995
> *Islamic Art and Indian, Himalayan and South-East Asian Art*, Sotheby's, London, 27 April 1995

Sotheby's, London, 24 April 1996
> *Oriental Manuscripts and Miniatures*, Sotheby's, London, 24 April 1996

Sotheby's, London, 17 October 1996
> *Islamic and Indian Art*, Sotheby's, London, Thursday 17 October 1996

Sotheby's, London, 8 May 1997
> *The Indian Sale*, Sotheby's, London, Thursday 8 May 1997

Sotheby's, London, 15 October 1998, 1
> *Arts of the Islamic World*, Sotheby's, London, Thursday 15 October 1998

Sotheby's, London, 22 April 1999, 1
> *Arts of the Islamic World*, Sotheby's, London, Thursday 22 April 1999

Sotheby's, London, 22 April 1999, 2
> *Islamic Art and Indian Painting*, Sotheby's, London, Thursday 22 April 1999

Sotheby's, London, 14 October 1999, 1
> *Arts of the Islamic World*, Sotheby's, London, Thursday 14 October 1999

Sotheby's, New York, 7 June 1994
> *Fine Jewelry*, Sotheby's, New York, June 7, 1994

Sotheby's, New York, 19 September 1996
> *Indian and Southeast Asian Art*, Sotheby's, New York, Thursday, September 19, 1996

Sotheby's, St Moritz, 16 and 17 February 2000
> *Magnificent Jewels*, Sotheby's, St Moritz, 16 and 17 February 2000

Spink, London, 1988
> Spink, Michael, ed., *Islamic and Hindu Jewellery*, exhibition/sale catalogue, Spink and Son Ltd, London, April 13th to May 6th 1988

Spink, London, 1994
> *Treasures of the Courts*, exhibition/sale catalogue, Spink and Son Ltd, London, 18th October–4th November 1994

Spink, London, October–November 1999
> *The Eye of the Courtier: Indian & Islamic Works of Art*, exhibition/sale catalogue, Spink, London, 11th October–12th November, 1999

Stronge 1996
> Stronge, Susan, 'The myth of the Timur Ruby', in *Jewellery Studies*, vol. 7 (1996)

Swarup 1996
> Swarup, Shanti, *Mughal Art: A Study in Handicrafts*, New Delhi, 1996

Welch 1985
> Welch, Stuart Cary, *India: Art and Culture 1300–1900*, New York, 1985

Zebrowski 1997, 1
> Zebrowski, Mark, *Gold, Silver & Bronze from Mughal India*, London, 1997

Zebrowski 1997, 2
> Zebrowski, Mark, 'Glamour and Restraint: Silver, Gold and Bronze from Mughal India', in *Hali Annual, First Under Heaven: The Art of Asia*, 1997

FURTHER READING

1 Works presenting significant amounts of important material relating to this catalogue

Archer, Mildred; Rowell, Christopher; and Skelton, Robert, *Treasures from India: The Clive Collection at Powis Castle*, New York, 1987

Balfour 1987 (see above)

Brand, Michael, and Lowry, Glenn D., *Akbar's India: Art from the Mughal City of Victory*, New York, 1985

[Copenhagen], *Islamiske våben i dansk privateje / Islamic Arms and Armour from Private Danish Collections*, catalogue of an exhibition at the David Collection, Copenhagen, 1982

Filliozat, J., and Pattabiramin, P. Z., *Parures divines du Sud de l'Inde*, Pondichéry, 1966

Haase, Claus-Peter; Kröger, Jens; and Lienert, Ursula, eds, *Oriental Splendour: Islamic Art from German Private Collections*, Hamburg, [1993]

Ivanov, A. A.; Lukonin, V. G.; and Smesova, L. S., *Oriental Jewelry from the Collection of the Special Treasury, the State Hermitage Oriental Department*, Moscow, 1984 (in Russian, brief catalogue entries in English)

Jenkins, Marilyn, and Keene, Manuel, *Islamic Jewelry in the Metropolitan Museum of Art*, New York, 1982

Keene, M., and Jenkins, M., '*Djawhar* ii, Jewel, jewelry', in *The Encyclopaedia of Islam*, New Edition, Supplement to vol. 2, fasc. 3–4 and 5–6, Leiden, 1981 and 1982, respectively

Meen, V. B., and Tushingham, A. D., *Crown Jewels of Iran*, Toronto and Buffalo, 1968

[Milan], *Gioielli dall'India, dai Moghul al Novecento*, Milan, 1996

Morley, Grace, 'On Applied Arts of India in Bharat Kala Bhavan', in *Chhavi: Golden Jubilee Volume*, Banaras, 1971

Nigam, M. L., *Jade Collection in the Salar Jung Museum*, Salar Jung Museum Board, Hyderabad (Deccan), 1979

Pal et al. 1989 (see above)

Ricketts, Howard, and Missillier, Philippe, *Splendeur des Armes orientales*, Paris, 1988

Skelton, Robert, 'Islamic and Mughal Jades', in *Jade*, ed. R. Keverne, London, 1991

Skelton, Robert, et al., *The Indian Heritage: Court Life and Arts under Mughal Rule*, London, 1982

Stronge, Susan, ed., *The Arts of the Sikh Kingdoms*, London, 1999

Stronge, Susan; Smith, Nima; and Harle, J. C., *A Golden Treasury: Jewellery from the Indian Subcontinent*, London and Middletown, New Jersey, 1988

Untracht, Oppi, *Traditional Jewelry of India*, London and New York, 1997

Weihreter, Hans, *Blumen des Paradieses: Der Fürstenschmuck Nordindiens*, Graz, 1997

Welch 1985 (see above)

Zebrowski 1997, 1 (see above)

2   Works incorporating specialized studies

Keene, Manuel, 'The Lapidary Arts in Islam: An Underappreciated Tradition', in *Expedition*, vol. 24, no. 1 (Fall, 1981)

Pinder-Wilson, Ralph, 'Jades from the Islamic World', in *Marg*, vol. XLIV, no. 2 (December 1992)

Skelton, Robert, 'The Shah Jahan Cup', in *V & A Museum Bulletin*, vol. 2, no. 3 (1966)

Skelton, Robert, 'The Relations between the Chinese and Indian Jade Carving Traditions', in *The Westward Influence of the Chinese Arts from the 14th to the 18th Century* (ed. William Watson), London, 1972

Skelton, Robert, 'Characteristics of Later Turkish Jade Carving', in Fehér, G., ed., *Proceedings of the Fifth International Conference of Turkish Art*, Budapest, 1978

Stronge, Susan, 'Colonel Guthrie's Collection: Jades of the Mughal Era', in *Oriental Art*, vol. XXXIX, no. 4 (Winter 1993–94)

Stronge, Susan, ed., *The Jewels of India*, Bombay [Mumbai], 1995

Stronge 1996 (see above)

3   Works of importance for general and background issues

Birdwood, Sir George, *The Industrial Arts of India*, London, [1880]

Egerton, Wilbraham (Lord Egerton of Tatton), *An Illustrated Handbook of Indian Arms; being a Classified and Descriptive Catalogue of the Arms Exhibited at the India Museum: with An Introductory Sketch of the Military History of India*, London, 1880

Skelton, Robert, 'Indian subcontinent, §VII, 11: Jade, agate and crystal', in *The Dictionary of Art*, vol. 15, London and New York, 1996

Skelton, Robert, 'Islamic art, §VIII, 8: Jade', in *The Dictionary of Art*, vol. 16, London and New York, 1996

4   Works incorporating related, supplementary and supportive material

Abdul Aziz, *The Imperial Treasury of the Indian Mughuls*, Delhi, 1972

Abū 'l-Faẓl 'Allāmī, *The Ā'īn-i Akbarī*, vol. III, trans. H. S. Jarrett, reprint edition, New Delhi, 1979

Atil, Esin, *The Age of Sultan Süleyman the Magnificent*, Washington, D.C., and New York, 1987

Baden Powell, B. H., *Handbook of the Manufactures and Arts of the Punjab*, Lahore, 1872

Begley, W. E., and Desai, Z. A., *Taj Mahal, The Illumined Tomb: An Anthology of Seventeenth-Century Mughal and European Documentary Sources*, Cambridge, Massachusetts, 1989

Brij Bhushan, Jamila, *Indian Jewellery, Ornaments, and Decorative Designs*, Bombay [Mumbai], 1964

Gascoigne, Bamber, *The Great Moghuls*, London, 1971

Jahāngīr, Nūr ad-Dīn Pādshāh (Mughal Emperor), *The Tūzuk-i-Jahāngīrī, or Memoirs of Jahāngīr*, trans. Alexander Rogers, ed. Henry Beveridge, London, 1909 and 1914, and various reprints, including New Delhi, 1989

Koch, Ebba, *Shah Jahan and Orpheus: The Pietre Dure Decoration and the Programme of the Throne in the Hall of Public Audiences at the Red Fort of Delhi*, Graz, 1988

Köseoğlu, Cengiz, and Rogers, J. M., *The Topkapı Saray Museum: The Treasury*, Boston, 1987

Latif, M., *Bijoux moghols/Mogol Juwelen/Mughal Jewels*, Brussels, 1982

Michell, George, and Zebrowski, Mark, *Architecture and Art of the Deccan Sultanates*, Cambridge (England), 1999

Rogers, J. M., and Ward, R. M., *Süleyman the Magnificent*, London, 1988

Speel, Erika, *Dictionary of Enamelling*, Aldershot (England), 1998

Stone, George Cameron, *A Glossary of the Construction, Decoration and Use of Arms and Armor, in All Countries and in All Times, Together with Some Closely Related Subjects*, New York, 1961 (reprint of 1934 original)

Untracht, Oppi, *Jewelry Concepts and Technology*, 2nd edn, New York, etc., 1985

Ward, Rachel, 'Goldsmiths' Work at the Court of Süleyman the Magnificent', in *Jewellery Studies*, vol. 4 (1990)

Watt, Sir George, *Indian Art at Delhi, 1903: Being the Official Catalogue of the Delhi Exhibition, 1902–1903*, London, 1904